Unmasking
Indian
Secularism

Unmasking Indian Secularism

WHY WE NEED A NEW HINDU-MUSLIM DEAL

HASAN SUROOR

Published by
Rupa Publications India Pvt. Ltd 2022
7/16, Ansari Road, Daryaganj
New Delhi 110002

Sales centres:
Allahabad Bengaluru Chennai
Hyderabad Jaipur Kathmandu
Kolkata Mumbai

Copyright © Hasan Suroor 2022

All rights reserved.

No part of this publication may be reproduced, transmitted,
or stored in a retrieval system, in any form or by any means,
electronic, mechanical, photocopying, recording or otherwise,
without the prior permission of the publisher.

The views and opinions expressed in this book are the author's
own and the facts are as reported by him which have been
verified to the extent possible, and the publishers are
not in any way liable for the same.

ISBN: 978-93-5520-406-6

First impression 2022

10 9 8 7 6 5 4 3 2 1

The moral right of the author has been asserted.

This book is sold subject to the condition that it shall not, by way of
trade or otherwise, be lent, resold, hired out, or otherwise circulated,
without the publisher's prior consent, in any form of binding
or cover other than that in which it is published.

For all those fellow Indians who value Indianness more than Hinduness or Muslimness—sadly, a shrinking tribe.

Contents

Introduction	*ix*
1. Breaking the Impasse	1
2. A Hindu Rashtra Can Also Be Secular	22
3. Secularism That Never Was	31
4. Limits of Mass Action: The Shaheen Bagh Syndrome	52
5. Hostage to Religious Nationalisms	82
6. Ordinary Indians Speak Out	104
Postscript: Will the Phoenix Rise Again?	142
Addenda	157
Index	189

Introduction

Watching the unravelling of Indian secularism, I am reminded of the popular Urdu poet and film lyricist Sahir Ludhianvi's famous line, '*Woh afsana jise anjaam tak laana na ho mumkin us-e ek khubsoorat mor de kar chodna achha* [When it's not possible to take a story to the desired conclusion, it's better to give it a dignified turn and end it]'. He was, of course, writing about unrequited love, how to get over it and move on.

But it is an equally apt prescription for the troubled *afsana* (tale) of our experiment with secularism which seemed like a good idea after the traumatic events of Partition, but 70 years on, it has come under sharp scrutiny amid widespread disillusionment with the way it has been practised over the years.

This book is a critical examination of the history of

India's post-Independence secular politics, including the somewhat controversial rationale of the Congress party behind choosing secularism as state policy. Whether a western concept of religious neutrality was suited to a historically deeply religious society has been a legitimate matter of concern. It has been said that it was destined to fail. Was the idea of declaring India a secular state really borne out of Nehru's innate liberalism? Alternatively, was it intended to score a political point over Hindu nationalists and the All-India Muslim League: an attempt by the Congress party to shame Mohammed Ali Jinnah, the founder of Pakistan, even as it laid foundations of a minority vote bank?

Meanwhile, instead of contributing to fostering communal harmony, as was intended, secularism has become a source of division, breeding resentment among the majority community that believes that it is disproportionately weighted in favour of minorities, especially Muslims. The incumbent Bharatiya Janata Party (BJP) and its allies, riding the current wave of Hindu nationalism, accuse secularists of minority 'appeasement' and peddling 'pseudo-secularism' for electoral gains.

Muslims and other minorities have their own reasons to be suspicious of the secular establishment. Far from benefiting from secularism, the minorities claim that their grievances and frustrations have been manipulated by the Congress party and other Centre-Left groups, and they have been used as proxies in the battles against Right-wing political rivals. Muslims are particularly angry, and their emphatic rejection of the Congress party underlines the strength of their dissatisfaction and resentment. Their withdrawal of support has been an existential blow to the Congress party, plunging it into terminal decline, which shows how reliant it had been on Muslim votes and lends credence to claims that it was simply interested in secularism as a route to building a Muslim 'vote bank'—presenting itself as their saviour against 'communal' Hindu groups.

The story of Indian secularism is a classic example of good intentions being derailed by misguided practices. Over the years, there has been enough post-mortem on why secularism has not worked and who's to blame. But we are where we are, and frankly, it makes no sense endlessly debating it. That will only generate more acrimony leading to more polatization. The effort now should be to ponder ways to find a way out of the mess. My aim here is to start a candid conversation about where we go from here.

It will not be easy, particularly for Muslims who might be required to make some hard choices in pursuit of an end to the insecurity and uncertainty they face about their future in India. More broadly, it will involve acknowledging certain facts that liberals may not find palatable: our historic failure to deliver on the promise of secularism and a profound change in Hindu public opinion, which, in recent years, has swung towards majoritarianism with the idea that Hindus have the first right over India becoming deeply ingrained, even among many liberals. Any sustainable solution will have to be within the context of these realities.

This is not a plea to abandon secularism altogether or suddenly embrace a theocratic Hindu state, but to look for a model that is more effectively in tune with contemporary political and social realities, and the current national mood—a settlement underpinned by realism rather than idealism. The effort should be to try and strike a balance between minority rights and the majority community's sensitivities, which it believes have been ignored in the name of secularism. The Hindu sense of grievance—real or imaginary—will have to be addressed in the larger interest of India's unity.

There's a mistaken notion that the only alternative to a secular state is a theocracy. I argue that a state can have an officially recognized religion—in India's case, it will be Hinduism—and yet remain secular in practice by treating all citizens as equal and making sure that their religious and civil rights are protected by law, as in many western liberal democracies, including Britain where the state is Christian, but government practices are secular. There exists a robust and strictly enforced equality law that ensures that nobody is discriminated against on the basis of their religion or ethnicity.

We can find successful examples of the British model or its variations in other countries across South Asia and the Muslim world. The book examines these models and argues that it would be a good starting point to study them as the basis for a new constitutional framework that would be seen to be fair to everyone without abandoning the essential elements of a secular society.

No debate on Hindu–Muslim relations would be complete without a reference to the role of nationalism in muddying the waters. The term 'nationalism' is tossed around a great deal these days and is considered a virtue and a badge of honour, but I trace the history of competing Hindu and Muslim cultural nationalisms to show how they have been used to divide people. Partition was a result of the clash between rival nationalisms, peddled by the Muslim League on the one hand and the Hindu Mahasabha and its allies on the other, both feeding on each other. I argue, on the basis of historical evidence, that both sides believed in the 'two-nation' theory, namely, Muslims and Hindus represented two separate civilizations and cultures, and never the twain shall meet. I explore how this worked on the ground with the Hindu Mahasabha actually collaborating with the Muslim League in opposing the Congress party even as the League campaigned for a separate Muslim homeland.

Muslim Activism

Notably, the last time we saw Muslim civil society mobilize in a significant way was when the League pushed for a separate Muslim state. Post Independence, Indian Muslims have shown little interest in mass action, and if they have, it has failed to take off because of a lack of credible leadership. The 2019 Shaheen Bagh protest against the Citizenship (Amendment) Act (CAA), 2019—the new citizenship law that is unapologetically discriminatory—was the first serious attempt by the community to organize, especially around a secular issue.

But its failure amid politically fuelled conspiracy theories about its aims underlined the limits of any mass action not supported by the vast majority of the population; in other words, which is restricted to a minority group.

The book analyses the genesis and evolution of the Shaheen Bagh movement and argues that for all the hype around it, the non-Muslim support for it remained restricted mostly to the usual liberal suspects—and towards the end, even some of that support fizzled out. The most revealing was the reluctance of the so-called secular parties to be seen supporting a Muslim protest for fear of being seen as anti-Hindu. In the end, the protesters were left high and dry, politically isolated and demoralized. This lack of support diminishes the possibility of a similar mobilization in the future, reinforcing the book's central argument that Muslims have few options other than seeking a new compact with the Indian state even if it means making some unpalatable concessions.

The book also offers a sense of the Muslim mood, with a section devoted to a cross-section of Muslim voices on the future of Hindu–Muslim relations. In the end, I reflect on the prevailing politically and culturally polarized climate—and how hard it has become to have a rational argument on Hindu–Muslim issues in such a climate. I draw on my own experience and explain why I've stopped arguing for fear of losing friends on both sides of the divide. Admittedly, it is not an optimistic note to end on, but here we are. And the quicker we start looking for a way out of this misery, the better it would be for all of us—and the nation at large.

1

Breaking the Impasse

*'No matter how hard the past is,
you can always begin again.'*

—Buddha

I am one of Salman Rushdie's metaphorical 'midnight's children', born on the morrow of Indian independence in a climate fraught with tense Hindu–Muslim relations in the wake of Partition. My generation of Hindus and Muslims grew up under the lingering shadow of Partition—two traumatized communities struggling to come to terms with its aftermath and, more importantly, struggling to reconcile with each other. Muslims carried additional baggage: the perception that even if they were not directly responsible for the country's division, they were still somehow complicit by virtue of being part of the larger Muslim 'ummah'; in other words, all Muslims were seen to bear some responsibility for the creation of Pakistan. The Right, which primarily consists of Hindu nationalists, perceived them as interlopers trying to have their cake (their 'own' homeland in Pakistan) and eat it too (a privileged life in India). On the other hand, Muslims felt they were being unfairly targeted for the sins of a few, and rather than being hailed for foregoing the safety of a Muslim state, they were portrayed as outsiders in the land of their ancestors. They felt anxious about their future.

It was against this background of mutual suspicion that the foundations of secular India were laid: not exactly propitious circumstances for experimenting with an alien and culturally sensitive concept that had proved controversial even in the lands of its birth—the liberal western democracies. Looking back, in the light of subsequent events, it is easy to question that decision. To be sure, it was a deliberate choice driven by Jawaharlal Nehru's westernized liberal outlook. There was no attempt to explore an indigenous model: a system that would have recognized the predominantly Hindu nature of Indian society without necessarily declaring India a Hindu state. But, as the cliché goes, hindsight is a wonderful thing.

But at the time, it seemed like a sensible choice even if not everyone, even in the Congress party, fully bought it. Primarily, it was designed to offer a sense of security and inclusion to a traumatized minority community concerned about its place in a Hindu majority state. But it was also a politically smart move to score moral brownie points over Pakistan. Here was a modern, democratic and secular India committing itself to protect its minorities and uphold the rule of law—thus asserting its higher moral and cultural values vis-à-vis a divisive theocracy founded on medieval-era values. There was certainly a hint of virtue-signalling in this 'inclusion'.

The more cynical view—initially confined to the Hindu Right, but shared more widely today—is that the whole secularism project was really an expedient by the Congress party to win over the Muslim community to cash in for its votes, an argument that the BJP would later use to successfully mobilize opinion against secularism, calling it 'pseudo-secularism'. It accused the Congress party of Muslim 'appeasement' to build a Muslim 'vote bank' while ignoring Hindu concerns. The efficacy of the secularism project is debatable, but the problem is that much of the debate has become too politicized to allow an objective evaluation. And it is not a recent change; it has been so for as long as I remember. Most of the discussion has been shaped by ideological and political party lines reducing it to a Liberal versus Right and, worse, Hindu versus Muslim issue. While advocates of secularism hail it as the only show in sight and are not willing even to consider any other alternative, its opponents find no advantage to it, rubbishing it as a western import and a liberal conspiracy against Hindus. Ordinary Hindus and Muslims have had little say in a discourse that has done so much to muddy community relations. If Hindu–Muslim relations are fraught today, it is largely because of the toxic political discourse over secularism dubbed a *tu-tu-main-main* (slanging match) between rival political parties.

Notwithstanding the much-vaunted *Ganga–Jamuni tehzeeb* (a fusion of Hindu-Muslim culture) and the liberal nostalgia for a 'Hindu–Muslim bhai, bhai' golden age, there is a long history of tensions between the two communities preceding Partition. But much of the post-Independence tensions and anti-Muslim sentiment can be traced to the heat generated by the political divide and the war of words over secularism; a war that critics of secularism, by being more vocal and belligerent, have won—convincing large swathes of the majority community that secularism is disadvantageous for them because it is predicated on the belief of prioritizing minority interests.

The drip-drip effect of this relentless campaign claiming that secularism has undermined 'Hindu pride' and made them feel like aliens in their 'own' land—encapsulated in the BJP's slogan, 'garv se kaho, "Hum Hindu hain" [say it with pride, "We are Hindu"]'—has led to a steady erosion of support for secularism even among liberal Hindus. There has been a profound transformation of Indian attitudes towards the so-called 'Muslim question' tellingly referred to by many as an 'unfinished business' leftover from Partition. Privately, even some relatively moderate Hindus talk of the need for a 'new deal' focusing more on Muslim integration than reinforcing a minority mindset which they believe is what the constitutional settlement did in 1950. It suggested to Muslims that they deserved a special status and protection from a marauding Hindu majority. The result, they argue, was to create false expectations and a sense of entitlement among Muslims on the one hand, and resentment among Hindus, on the other. It didn't help either side and instead sowed the seeds of divisions that were then used by the Hindu Right to advance its political agenda.

In the aftermath of the 2002 communal violence in Gujarat, a group of left-liberal scholars—among them Martha Nussbaum, Christophe Jaffrelot and Neera Chandhoke—contributed to a volume, *Will Secular India Survive?*, edited by late historian Mushirul Hasan. Despite its funereal title, reflecting the widespread mood of doom and gloom that prevailed at the time, the book was remarkably upbeat about the future of Indian secularism. While not downplaying the threat it faced from Right-wing Hindu and Muslim groups, the writers believed that it was still the only viable show in town, given India's cultural and religious diversity. Since then, however, some have started to row back on their optimism.[1]

Prof. Chandhoke now acknowledges that 'secularism is in crisis', and that shoots of a 'post-secular age' are sprouting all over the world. There is need, she argues, to 're-examine' the concept.

> Secularism, however, is in crisis, having been subjected to overuse. While a 'thin' and limited concept, secularism, in India for example, has had to shoulder the onerous task of nation building, take on the construction of a uniform civil code, bear responsibility for reorganizing and equalizing hierarchical relationships within religious communities, and even stand in for democracy. Unable to bear the weight of too many political projects, it shows signs of imploding. The west, in the meantime, seems to have given up on secularism and declared post-secularism. Moments of crisis provide an opportunity to re-examine a concept, clarify what it means and stands for, what the political context of the concept is. This moment can be productive because it compels us to reconsider the foundational presumptions of secularism and rescue this beleaguered concept not only from its opponents, but also its ardent supporters.[2]

---

[1] Hasan, Mushirul (ed.) *Will Secular India Survive?*, The University Press Limited (UPL), Dhaka, 2004, pages.

[2] Chandhoke, Neera. 'Rethinking Secularism: A View From India', *global-e*, Vol. 10, No. 9, 14 February 2014, https://bit.ly/3HwI3Sq. Accessed on 24 February 2022.

Another liberal political and social scientist, Rajeev Bhargava of the Delhi-based Centre for the Study of Developing Societies (CSDS) who has written extensively on the subject, fears that secularism is doomed in its current form and the only way to save it is a radical 'course correction'. But that will require 'self-reflexivity and self-criticism' on the part of secularists who, according to him, are as much responsible for the state it is in as its 'external' enemies.

Delivering the 2020 Asghar Ali Engineer Lecture, he said that the threat to secularism predated the coming to power of the Narendra Modi government though it has now become more serious. The fact was that secularism had long been 'facing an internal threat in the sense that, the myopia, neglect, complacency, propensity for ritual hyperbole, weakness of will or failure of nerve of its proponents has also undermined it'.[3]

> This internal threat has also been political, social, cultural and intellectual... Those who defend secularism have frequently lost sight of the whole point behind a secular state, what secularism is for. More specifically, they do not fully understand what it was that gave Indian secularism its point and what made it.[4]

---

[3]Prof. Rajeev Bhargava on 'Does Indian Secularism have a Future?', YouTube, https://bit.ly/3ppOVuN. Accessed on 24 February 2022.
[4]Ibid.

This is open and vocal repudiation from a liberal proponent of secularism. It breaks a liberal taboo against acknowledging the failure of our experiment with secularism because doing so would mean admitting a historic failure. But, as Prof. Chandhoke's candid observations illustrate, they are gradually coming round to the admission, however cautiously or grudgingly. There is no shame in accepting that India has changed and the 1950s Nehruvian model of western-style liberal/secular democracy is no longer in sync with today's 'new' India. John Maynard Keynes, the great economist, famously said: 'When the facts change, I change my mind. What do you do, sir?' The old liberal order is struggling around the world in the face of resurgent ethnic nationalism. So, in a way, we're all in it together when it comes to adjusting to new political fashions. Rather than keeping up the appearance that nothing has changed, it would be more honest to try and adapt to the changing political landscape. What we need is a new constitutional settlement between Hindus and Muslims—an arrangement that would reflect the altered national mood.

The truth is that secularism, as practised over the past 70 years, has not worked, not only for Hindus, but also for Muslims—a fact often ignored. There's an assumption that being in the minority, Muslims are ipso facto cheerleaders for secularism. The reality is rather different. Muslims have no particular attachment to the idea of secularism per se except as constitutional insurance against discrimination on religious grounds. They would have as happily gone along with any other arrangement—even a benign Hindu Rashtra which provided them security and dignity—that offered them the same protections as were promised by secularism. Remember, Muslims never campaigned for an explicitly secular India at the time of Independence, nor was their decision to stay in India necessarily influenced by the political nature of the state. They chose to remain, mainly because India was their ancestral land and they wished to continue to live here. Some held back from migrating to Pakistan because of economic reasons, and the lack of education and professional skills needed to start afresh in a new land. There were a number of reasons why they chose to remain in India, and certainly, the promise of equal rights helped, but secularism was not a decisive factor.

The point I'm trying to labour is that secularism holds no special sanctity for Muslims; it's just a means to an end, the end being a desire to live in peace and dignity. But after 70 years of secularism, that remains elusive. It hasn't delivered what it promised on the tin. Far from doing them any good, it has instead made them a target of backlash from Right-wing Hindu nationalists. The wholesale Muslim rejection of the Congress party and other assorted self-appointed secular saviours is a stark reflection of their deep disillusionment with the way secular political establishment has practised secularism.

Indeed, I've noticed an alarming trend among some

young Muslims put off by secular parties: they have cultivated a quiet admiration for populist Muslim demagogues like Asaduddin Owaisi of the All India Majlis-e-Ittehadul Muslimeen (AIMIM). They see him as a more authentic champion of their cause than their secular allies have proved to be. An argument I frequently hear is: 'we tried secularists and were let down; now let's give these guys a chance and see how it goes.' It echoes the justification used by disillusioned Hindu Congress supporters to defend their embrace of the BJP. Owaisi admirers remain a minority, but a community feeling under siege, let down by secular friends, and fearful of its future can easily become desperate enough to seek solace in unlikely places.

However, to cut to the chase, we are where we are; and endless post-mortems will not take us anywhere except to more finger-pointing, more acrimony and more bitterness. It's time we started looking for a way out of the impasse. This means: stop obsessing about the past, take stock of where we are, and see how best to retrieve the situation before it worsens. Admittedly, given the current state of Hindu–Muslim relations, this will not be easy and require considerable compromises from both sides, particularly from the Muslim community, because ultimately, its future is at stake.

Unfortunately, it doesn't have the luxury of too many choices even as the current situation—irrespective of how it came about—is not sustainable. The community is politically isolated. Even its traditional allies—Congress and others—have started to abandon it, sensing that it has become a political liability in a climate where any overt support for Muslims is liable to be seen as being anti-Hindu. The outcome of the Shaheen Bagh protests showed both the extent of its political isolation and the limits of mass action at a time when anti-Muslim sentiment has never been so pronounced. It has become a cliché to say that Indian Muslims are at the 'crossroads': I have been hearing this for as long as I can remember. Even in the so-called 'good old days' of Hindu–Muslim relations, they were portrayed as a community lost at the crossroads of its destiny. But if ever that description was true, it is today: the decisions Muslims take today will define their future in India for generations to come.

There are only two choices before them; either remain bogged down in an endless debate about the past—who did what to whom and who is to blame for the current impasse—or to take a good hard look at their circumstances and start exploring a pragmatic and more effective approach. For the Hindu community, too, despite what the votaries of a Hindu Rashtra might claim, the reality is that it will not be easy to turn back the clock, uprooting the very foundations of the modern Indian state, and to replace it with a theocracy—something for which India has criticized other countries. Constitutional hurdles apart, it will be hard to sell it politically—and diplomatically—if sought to be pushed through without visible popular mandate such as through a referendum or credible nationwide public campaign calling for such a radical change. One way of seeking legitimacy will be for the BJP to include it in its election manifesto and seek votes promising a Hindu state—as it did over building a Ram Mandir on the site of Babri Masjid.

But beyond the far-Right Hindutva bubble, will the mainstream Sangh Parivar leadership have the appetite for such a controversial move, given the potential reputational damage it is likely to do to India's image as South Asia's sole pillar of secular democracy in a region engulfed by religious and cultural strife? Truth be told, both communities are constrained by objective factors and are not really in a position to have it all their way: neither an all-singing-all-dancing secular utopia sought by Muslims, nor an in-your-face Hindu Rashtra sought by Hindu nationalists.

Therefore, any serious search for a solution will require a willingness on both sides to come together without preconditions and be ready to make compromises. It needs to be reiterated that Muslims should be prepared to forego more because—as I have argued before—they have more at stake, nothing short of their children and grandchildren's future in India. They have nowhere else to go; indeed, they don't want to go anywhere and wish to continue to live in India as they have for centuries. Securing a future in which they will not be discriminated against, feel safe, and be treated with respect is, thus, an existential issue—and to resolve it amicably, even if it means having to run an extra mile, should be the goal of the community at large.

That Muslims surrender unconditionally to the Hindu Right is not the defense to be made here. That would not be consistent with my own idea of dignity and respect, but it is important not to forget what is at stake for them. And when the stakes are so high and the balance of power is so heavily tilted against you, there is nothing to be ashamed of in going the extra mile to secure your future.

So, what might a re-examination of secularism entail for Muslims in real terms? For starters, a frank acceptance of the demise of secularism without further ado as to its causes or who is to blame. But, more importantly, a recognition of a marked pro-majoritarian tilt in the national mood. The view that the majority community has the first right over India has become deeply ingrained and is here to stay whether the Narendra Modi government stays or goes. The new citizenship law, which explicitly excludes Muslims and Christians from the category of minorities persecuted in other countries and entitled to Indian citizenship, effectively formalizes the conflation of India with Hindus. The optimistic liberal belief that all they need is to defeat the BJP government and it will be back to business as usual is a fantasy. The sense of Hindu nationalism has become very real in recent years, and it will be hard to roll it back. The genie, as it were, has been let out of the bottle and there is no point pretending that it can be put back even if there was a political will to do so, of which, there is no evidence. It is not in the nature of genies to scurry back into the hole. Hoping for any other outcome just because it is fantastical will only prolong the agony and lead to more disappointment at the end of the day.

The writing on the wall is clear, and to ignore it is to bury one's head in the sand. Centrist parties, including the Congress, have already changed their tune, taking care to tone down their secular rhetoric and instead stress their Hinduness. Rahul Gandhi, the political scion of the Nehru–Gandhi family showed off his janeu (sacred thread) and talked about his gotra in the lead up to the 2019 general elections to woo the Hindu vote.[5] 'Rahul flaunts his "janeu", pitches a journey to Kailash Mansarovar as the high point of his "Shiv bhakti", criss-crosses temples across India during elections, sports a "tilak" on his forehead and tells the head priest in Pushkar that he is a Dattatreya Kaul Brahmin… The Congress has been desperate to claim the Hindu legacy,' wrote Naghma Sahar ahead of the 2019 general elections.[6]

Speaking in Parliament, after the election, Modi boasted that no political party had had the courage to even mention the word 'secularism' during the campaign; and he was

---

[5] '"My gotra is Dattatreya, I am a Kashmiri Brahmin": Rahul Gandhi in Pushkar', *The Economic Times*, 27 November 2018, https://bit.ly/3vFCwXu. Accessed on 2 March 2022.

[6] Sahar, Naghma. 'Rahul Gandhi revealing his gotra is the final blow to "secular" politics', *DailyO*, 30 November 2018, https://bit.ly/3ppFDim. Accessed on 24 February 2022.

right.[7] Lest I should be accused of tarring the entire Hindu community with the saffron brush, I must stress that there's still a pretty solid core of liberal Hindus who have actively resisted the Hinduization of India and continue to do so. But they are becoming increasingly marginalized amid creeping majoritarianism flowing from a widespread belief that Hindu sensitivities have been ignored for too long in the name of secularism. And this Hindu sense of grievance—real or imaginary—will have to be addressed in the larger interest of good community relations.

The view that only minorities are entitled to air their grievances and that the Hindus are too privileged to complain by virtue of being in the majority is misplaced. It is largely informed by our experience of majoritarian theocracies such as in the Arab world and authoritarian countries like China. But there are multicultural democracies where dominant groups can often feel left out as a 'neutral' state tries to protect and promote minority interests. For example, in the predominantly white United Kingdom (UK) and United States of America (USA), large sections of white working classes feel neglected and resent the fact that their governments spend so much time talking about the interests of racial and ethnic minorities. Whether their sense of grievance is exaggerated or even imaginary is

---

[7]Mustafa, Faizan. 'Minorities, Too, Are Fed Up With This Façade of Secularism', *The Indian Express*, 21 March 2020, https://bit.ly/3MafQo4. Accessed on 24 February 2022.

immaterial, what should worry us is the danger of ignoring these grievances and allowing them to fester. We have seen how populist nationalists in the US and Europe have exploited these to target ethnic minorities, blaming them for the 'plight' of native white groups and fuelling xenophobia. The Modi phenomenon itself is a product of this sense of grievance among Hindus.

Having said that, there should be no room under the new compact for entertaining abstract grievances or demands around religious and cultural 'sensitivities' such as those that led to the demolition of Babri Masjid and the controversy surrounding Salman Rushdie's book, *The Satanic Verses*. Both communities are guilty of touting spurious grievances and making demands citing religious or cultural sensitivities. The 'new' grown-up India should have an unambiguously no-nonsense approach to upholding the rule of law. Matters of 'faith' that can't be tested in a court of law should have no place in a rule-based modern democracy. The good news is that a debate on the need to rethink Hindu–Muslim relations is already underway in the Muslim community disillusioned with the current secular order. Notwithstanding their public invocation of the Nehruvian idea of India, there's a quiet Muslim acknowledgement that the post-Partition settlement has broken down. And that a new order is in town, and for the sake of their own physical and economic security, they will need to 'fit in'. To re-emphasize the point made earlier, altered political realities and national mood require a new settlement between Muslims and the Indian state.

A number of creative ideas are being tossed around. Remarkably, these include accepting the idea of a Hindu Rashtra—something even most Hindus don't feel comfortable with. Among its Muslim proponents are a number of legal luminaries such as constitutional scholar, Faizan Mustafa, vice chancellor of NALSAR University, Hyderabad. 'But if Hindus really feel threatened from [sic] Muslims and Christians, we must address their concerns and not shy away from discussing the possibility of a Hindu rashtra,' he wrote in a widely debated article in *The Indian Express*.[8] 'Minorities, too, are now fed up with this façade of secularism, with all state institutions tilting towards one religion. Perhaps some kind of Hindu Rashtra can help us bring peace and save the country from the path of self-destruction,' he argued.[9]

Minorities, he assured them, need not worry too much about it; 'Just like several other modern theocracies, a Hindu Rashtra could guarantee substantial rights to religious minorities. It will not be based on the Manusmriti and will uphold modern ideas of human rights, particularly the right to equality and non-discrimination.' He has made light of legal hurdles, arguing that it will 'merely require a 15-judge Supreme Court bench to overrule the basic structure limitation on the Parliament's power to amend

---

[8]Ibid.
[9]Ibid.

the Constitution'—a reference on the bar on Parliament to change those provisions of the Constitution that are deemed essential to its 'basic structure'.[10] Secularism is one of them.

A few years ago, it would have been unthinkable for a prominent Muslim scholar to publicly propagate for the Hindu Rashtra—and for a leading national newspaper to publish it: the writer would have been declared persona non grata in their own community, accused of selling out to the Rashtriya Swayamsevak Sangh (RSS), and the paper would have been dubbed communal for promoting such an idea. However, it's a measure of the temper of the times that Mustafa's article has resonated widely in the Muslim community, with many complimenting him for giving voice to their views. The fact is that the idea of Hindu Rashtra has become a topic of kitchen-table discussion in Muslim homes, the dominant view being that a Hindu theocratic state will be a more honest alternative to the current charade of secularism; under a Hindu Rashtra minorities will be clearer about their status making it easier for them to adjust their expectations, which might ultimately lead to better Hindu–Muslim relations.

There are several successful models of modern theocratic democracies where the state has an established religion, but all religious groups are treated as equal. These include

---

[10]Ibid.

Christian states of UK, Ireland, Greece, the Jewish state of Israel—the neighbouring Islamic state of Bangladesh and the Buddhist state of Sri Lanka. At least two major Southeast Asian Muslim-majority states—Malaysia and Indonesia—successfully combine elements of theocracy with a system of democratic rights for all citizens irrespective of their religion. These models are discussed in more detail in the following chapter.

But right now, the most important task for those of us who are serious about bridging the Hindu–Muslim divide is to start a dispassionate and grown-up debate on the way forward—framed, not as an argument for a Hindu Rashtra, but as an attempt to break the current impasse and explore alternatives to our experiment with secularism that, for all its good intentions, has failed to satisfy either the majority community or minority faith groups. People must be presented with alternatives and invited to examine them in the cold light of the fact that the current situation is untenable and, if allowed to fester, would only benefit radicals in both communities, leading to more communal tensions, possibly, even irrevocable violence. Before it's too late, sensible and peace-loving Hindus and Muslims—and I firmly believe that the overwhelming majority on both sides are sensible and peace-loving—must seize the initiative to find a dignified way out of the quagmire of worsening community relations.

But it will require party politics, sectarian opportunism,

and, crucially, the Left–Right intellectual divide (not to mention liberal political correctness) to take second place to the more pressing task of settling, once and for all, the long-standing contentious issue of the status of minorities in a Hindu-majority India through and mutual consent. And a big part of this dialogue will involve creating conditions for a sustained and productive dialogue between the communities. Even as I believe Muslims will need to sacrifice more, a successful breakthrough can be achieved only when both sides reach out to each other in a spirit of accommodation. The responsibility of improving Hindu–Muslim relations cannot be left to one community alone. It takes two to tango. For any Muslim initiative to take off, much less succeed, the BJP and the RSS will need to respond with a measure of reciprocity, indeed, even magnanimity, to reach out to minorities, offering them a deal they cannot refuse. It will make the task of pro-change Muslim campaigners much easier, not to mention, give the majority community a moral high ground.

Meanwhile, before I wrap up, it is worth reiterating and re-emphasizing the thrust of my central argument, namely, that there is no ignominy in acknowledging our historic failure to make a success of our experiment with secularism. As pointed out before, history is littered with corpses of well-intentioned political projects. Vladimir Lenin's model of socialism failed, but that doesn't detract from his brave attempt to transform a poor peasant society into a modern, progressive and egalitarian nation. The problem was a refusal to acknowledge when it failed to work and take corrective measures; by the time they did, it was too late. Look at what has happened to Pakistan because it remains in denial that Jinnah's idea of a liberal Muslim state was a non-starter. In India, it's still not too late to be upfront and make a course correction.

Once again, the words of Sahir Ludhianvi ring true—when it is not possible to take a story to its logical conclusion, it's better to introduce a twist in the tale and move on from there.

2

A Hindu Rashtra Can Also Be Secular

'Let us move forward with strong and active faith.'
—Franklin D. Roosevelt

The mere mention of a Hindu Rashtra tends to invoke images of a majoritarian jackboot regime in which—like in Pakistan—minorities will be pushed back to the last row, stripped of their freedom to practise their religion, forced to be governed by a uniform civil code, and banished from public life in addition to being subjected to other indignities. While it's true that there are Hindu zealots whose concept of a Hindu Rashtra is close to this image, in reality, it needn't be like this. The problem is that the idea of a Hindu state has never been seriously debated, and our imagined image of it comes entirely from its extreme interpretations—like the radical interpretations of the idea of an Islamic state.

So, let's see what a majoritarian Hindu state could look like, stripped of its extreme caricature? A modern Hindu state committed to democracy and the rule of law, both of which presuppose equal rights for all citizens irrespective of their faith or ethnicity, shouldn't worry minorities too much. On the face of it, all that will happen is that the state which has no religion at the moment will adopt Hinduism as its official creed. There are fears that this will automatically lead to a sweeping Hinduization of India with non-Hindus reduced to second-class status.

These fears emanate mostly from the experience of minorities in authoritarian Islamic theocracies, but the experience of western Christian democracies has been very different. There is a great deal of ignorance about the nature of a denominational state, and it is widely confused with a theocratic state. But a state with an official religion is not the same thing as a theocracy. A state can have a government-sanctioned religion, but unlike in a theocracy, the state is not controlled by clergy and is not governed by religious laws. For example, a state might recognize Islam as its official religion but doesn't have to be necessarily governed by sharia and is free to pursue secular policies if it so chooses to do. Both Iran and Bangladesh are Muslim states, but while Iran is a theocracy, Bangladesh is not, though its state religion is Islam.

The UK is the most widely cited example of an avowedly denominational state, which, in practice, is a flourishing multi-religious and multicultural democracy. It has an established Church—the Church of England, whose bishops sit in the House of Lords. No other faith is represented in Parliament. Parliamentary proceedings begin with a Christian prayer. The Queen is both the head of state and supreme governor of the Church of England. One of the monarch's titles is Defender of the Faith. The Archbishop of Canterbury, spiritual head of the Church of England, is a highly revered figure, actively engaged in public life. British prime ministers routinely remind people that it is a 'Christian country' and urge them to uphold 'Christian values'. The only official holidays apart from bank holiday are meant to mark Christian events—Easter and Christmas.

But the British society and its official institutions—bureaucracy, judiciary, police, educational system—are secular. All citizens, irrespective of their religion, race, or ethnicity, are considered equal and their rights are guaranteed by strictly enforced equality laws. Their breach is a legal offence. In 2010, various disparate laws were brought together under a comprehensive, umbrella UK Equality Act which provides a legal framework to 'protect the rights of individuals and advance equality of opportunity for all... and promotes a fair and more equal society'.[1] It encompasses the following previous legislations guaranteeing protection from discrimination on a range of grounds, including on the basis of 'religion or belief':

- The Equal Pay Act 1970
- The Sex Discrimination Act 1975
- The Race Relations Act 1976
- The Disability Discrimination Act 1995
- The Employment Equality (Religion or Belief) Regulations 2003
- The Employment Equality (Sexual Orientation) Regulations 2003
- The Employment Equality (Age) Regulations 2006
- The Equality Act 2006, Part 2
- The Equality Act (Sexual Orientation) Regulations 2007

Nearer home, there is Bangladesh—a Muslim-majority nation with Islam as the state religion. But freedom of religion is constitutionally guaranteed, and, at least theoretically, all citizens enjoy equal rights irrespective of religion. Likewise, Malaysia is a Muslim-majority country with Islam as the officially recognized state religion. But the Federal Constitution guarantees equal rights to people of all

---

[1] 'Equality Act 2010', legislation.gov.uk, 8 April 2010, https://bit.ly/3hSlKfq. Accessed on 8 March 2022.

religions. Islamic prohibitions, such as the ban on alcohol consumption, apply only to Muslims and are not imposed on non-Muslims. Then there's the Jewish state of Israel that recognizes more than a dozen non-Jewish religious communities, all of which are allowed to practise their own religious family laws. Muslims constitute the largest religious minority accounting for around 14 per cent of the overall population.[2] They are free under the law to vote, practise religion and run for Parliament. They are governed by Islamic laws and it is claimed that sharia courts have more powers than Jewish, Christian and Druze courts with their verdicts treated on a par with those of civil courts. Many Arabs are part of the Israeli government and are represented in Parliament and the judiciary, including the Supreme Court.

These are just a few models of modern democracies that successfully combine elements of theocracy with secular practices. There is no universal, one-size-fits-all model, and specific practices vary from country to country, but all of them have one thing in common: the primacy of the dominant religion is officially recognized in some form. Tunisia, Greece and Ireland are some of the better-known examples of such a model.

So, the idea that it must be a binary choice between an all-out theocratic state and 'pure' secularism (you are either in Saudi Arabia or France) is a fallacy. In fact, a majority

---

[2]'Israel's Religiously Divided Society', Pew Research Centre, 8 March 2016, https://pewrsr.ch/3vPwGTD. Accessed on 3 March 2022.

of modern, newly independent democracies are hybrid in nature and combine elements of majoritarianism with secular practices. We will find ourselves spoilt for choice once we seriously get down to finding an alternative to our current arrangement.

RSS chief, Mohan Bhagwat, has said that a 'Hindu Rashtra' does not mean it has no place for Muslims as this concept is inclusive of all faiths and religions. He insists that the RSS is 'not anti-minorities and doesn't propose to change the framework of the Constitution', as alleged by the Opposition.

'We think everyone must abide by the Constitution... The RSS has never gone against the Constitution. (Sure), the words secular and socialist were added later, but now they are there,' he said in a series of lectures as part of what was billed as an 'outreach' exercise aimed at those not familiar with its aims.[3]

The proof of the pudding, of course, is in the taste. So, we shall see. Perhaps a beginning can be made by setting up an independent commission of eminent jurists, intellectuals and community leaders drawn from across the religious and cultural spectrum to study the various models and decide which would suit us best or pick-and-mix best practices from different sources. Their final choice or preferably a shortlist

---

[3]Ramachandran, Smriti Kak. 'No Hindu Rashtra Without Muslims, Hindutva Based on Unity in Diversity: Mohan Bhagwat', *Hindustan Times*, 18 September 2018, https://bit.ly/3hFIYFM. Accessed on 3 March 2022.

of favourites may be put out for public consultation through town-hall debates, public meetings and inviting people to send their views to the commission, or the proposals could be put to a public referendum before they are brought before the lawmakers. Parliament may then vote on the final package shaped by nationwide consultation.

By the way, India would not be the first country to swap existing constitutional arrangements for another one. It has become routine among newly independent countries, though mainly those that suffer from political instability. Bangladesh was founded in 1972 as a secular democracy modelled on the Indian system, but in 1977, secularism was removed from the Constitution by the then president, Ziaur Rahman's regime replacing it with a statement of 'absolute trust and faith in Almighty Allah'.[4] In 1988, Islam was declared as the state religion of Bangladesh. In a further twist in 2010, the Bangladesh Supreme Court restored secularism as one of the basic tenets of the Constitution but stated that Islam remained its state religion. Constitutionally, it's now a secular state, but with Islam as the state religion. In practice, secularism in Bangladesh has weakened over the years, and Right-wing Muslims have become more active, posing a threat both to non-Muslims and moderate Muslims.

Meanwhile, as an aside, it is interesting to note that a country that comes closest to the sort of crisis secularism

---

[4]Riaz, Ali and Rahman, Mohammad Sajjadur (eds). *Routledge Handbook of Contemporary Bangladesh*, Routledge, 2016, p. 42.

is facing in India is Turkey. It has a much longer history of constitutional secularism than India, but in recent years it has come under pressure from the Muslim Right represented by President Recep Tayyip Erdoğan's ruling party, Justice and Development Party (AKP)—Turkey's equivalent of the BJP—to Islamize the country. Under his leadership, Islam and Islamic symbols have become more prominent in public life, for example, all primary and secondary schools must offer religious teaching mostly focusing on the Sunni sect of Islam, though other religions are also covered briefly. His controversial decision last summer to order the reclassification of Hagia Sophia—a sixteenth-century Byzantine structure, originally built as a church, which was later converted into a mosque, and then, a museum—is part of Erdoğan's Islamization project. The move provoked international condemnation, including sharp criticism from the United Nations Educational, Scientific and Cultural Organization (UNESCO).

Like in India, some of the backlash against secularism in Turkey can be traced to the way intolerant secularists used it to target religion and any form of religiosity. Kemal Atatürk, the aggressively secular founder of modern Turkey, banned Islamic cultural practices, such as wearing a fez cap or keeping a beard, in favour of 'secular' western sartorial fashions. Secularism became a stick to beat religion with, in a traditionally religious society. Even as Turkish secularism was hailed by liberals around the world, at home it stoked anger which was mined by Islamists to advance their agenda leading to the formation of AKP in 2001 by activists of disparate sectarian groups.

But the big difference between the Indian and Turkish situations is that Turkey doesn't have a substantial non-Muslim minority population, so any change will not affect many people, whereas in India, millions of people—among them, 200 million Muslims—will be affected if their status is suddenly downgraded because of radical constitutional changes. Hence, the need to tread cautiously and with sensitivity. We cannot afford to get it wrong a second time.

3

Secularism That Never Was

'In my beginning is my end...'

—T.S. Eliot

A question frequently asked when debating Indian secularism is: so, what went wrong? How did we come to this? The question assumes that it was all wonderful once; different communities lived in peace and harmony, and secularism flourished. Currently, there's a wave of nostalgia in liberal circles for the 'good old days' of Hindu–Muslim unity. It's amusing to read and hear sentimental accounts of my liberal Hindu and Muslim friends invoking images of a lost paradise because my own memories of the past 70 years or so are somewhat different. I remember growing up in a climate of perpetual tension, strife and violent Hindu–Muslim flare-ups referred to simply as 'communal riots' without mentioning the communities involved even though everyone knew who they were.

As a young reporter in the 1970s, I wrote accounts of many of these 'incidents'. So frequent were these clashes that most major newspapers had teams of reporters on call 24/7, just in case one of the many hotspots (Aligarh, Meerut, Moradabad, Muzaffarnagar, Kanpur or Muslim neighbourhoods of Old Delhi) exploded again. My memories are of attempts to undermine Muslim institutions; of running battles over Aligarh Muslim University's (AMU) minority character; of delegitimization of Urdu language; of Muslims abused as fifth columnists; of routine anti-Muslim discrimination in jobs; of Muslims being denied houses for rent by Hindu landlords; and of Muslim areas being described as 'mini-Pakistan', and all this, long before the era of demolition of Babri Masjid, or 2002 Gujarat riots in which hundreds of Muslims were massacred. To be honest, it has been one very long haul for Muslims in secular India. There never was a 'golden age' of Hindu–Muslim relations with much of the history of independent India marked by mutual prejudice and suspicion.

The only difference between 'then' and 'now' is that

the political and public discourse has since become coarser with the old façade of civility gone. Whereas once Hindu landlords felt the need to invent an excuse to turn down a Muslim tenant, now housing associations openly declare a 'no Muslims' policy as widely reported in the media. A comprehensive study published in 2021 revealed the extent of 'exclusion' Muslims face in renting houses in India's most diverse and ostensibly cosmopolitan cities, including Delhi and Mumbai.[1] 'Homeowners and cooperative housing societies refuse to rent them apartments. Discrimination in housing on the basis of religion has become so commonplace that it is practically hidden in plain sight,' said the study conducted by the Housing Discrimination Project run by an interdisciplinary team of researchers. It found that in Delhi and Mumbai, 'brokers consistently conceded that they refuse certain prospective tenants, especially Muslims'. The report continued that, 'in some cases, they revealed their own biases during interviews. In numerous instances, they said they felt Muslim tenants could be a "liability"'; the report quoted one Hindu broker as saying that 'he did not discriminate among Muslims—he simply refuses all Muslim clients. "No landlord will agree to keep them," he claimed, "so why should I waste time?"'[2]

---

[1]Bhat, Mohsin Alam. 'Bigotry At Home: How Delhi, Mumbai Keep Muslim Tenants Out', Article-14, 11 February 2021, https://bit.ly/3stOv8B. Accessed on 24 February 2022.
[2]Ibid.

Signs of majoritarianism are all around us. And the controversial CAA, which pointedly excludes Muslims from a list of persecuted minorities who will be entitled to seek Indian citizenship, and plans to deport Muslims who don't have documents to prove that they are Indian citizens even if they were born and brought up in India, is simply an extreme manifestation of the majoritarian trend that had long been simmering under the surface.

Gandhi was once asked what he thought of western civilization. He famously replied that it was a 'good idea'. With less irony, the same can be said of Indian secularism: it was a good idea—a bold, progressive vision of bringing together a diverse and divided nation after the trauma of Partition. There was no regional precedent for such a project, and India was to become the first full-fledged secular democracy not only in South Asia but most of the non-western world, though, notably, the term 'secular' was not to feature in the Constitution until a quarter of a century later. It was in 1976—during the 21-month Emergency (1975–77)—that the Indira Gandhi government brought it in through a controversial constitutional amendment that overnight turned India from a 'sovereign democratic republic' to a 'sovereign, socialist secular democratic republic'. The 42nd Amendment, through which it was done, remains a bone of political and legal contention to this day. To be clear, the Amendment—dubbed the 'Constitution of Indira'—was not explicitly designed to make these changes. They were part of a bigger package of the most sweeping changes made to the Constitution in its history aimed at clipping the wings of the judiciary, including the Supreme Court, which was stripped of its powers to pronounce upon the constitutional validity of any law. Instead, it gave Parliament unrestricted power to amend any parts of the Constitution without judicial review. Some of the more controversial changes were later reversed by the Janata Party government—which came to power after the elections held following the Emergency in 1977—but those relating to socialism and secularism remain intact despite threats by successive BJP governments to remove them.

However, while they remain on paper, both concepts have since been heavily compromised with not even a little help from the Congress itself. While socialism went out the window with the 1990s sweeping economic liberalization introduced by the then finance minister, Dr Manmohan Singh under the leadership of late Prime Minister P.V. Narasimha Rao, ending the state monopoly of national resources, secularism took a beating from resurgent Hindu nationalism—propelled, in part, by the Congress party's ineptness combined with its political expediency. Mrs Gandhi's own intention behind the decision to insert 'secularism' into the Constitution out of the blue was a gratuitous political move. It was meant as a poke in the eye for her Right-wing political rivals she deemed 'communal', but instead, she ended up handing them further ammunition to accuse her of 'minorityism'. They also used it to fuel the simmering Hindu resentment over the Congress party's perceived pro-Muslim-pro-minorities tilt.

As it happened, even Muslims were not impressed by what they saw as a show of faux secularism after having suffered some of the worst atrocities during the Emergency. Thousands of Muslim residents of Delhi's Turkman Gate area were rendered homeless and lost their livelihood as they were forcibly removed from the area, which had been their home for generations, to far-flung new 'colonies' that lacked basic amenities and work opportunities. Their old homes were bulldozed in the name of urban development and the area's 'beautification'. Those who resisted were fired upon by police, reportedly leading to many deaths. The media was barred from covering the incident. An official count of the number of people killed in the firing is still not available but in anecdotal accounts it was widely described as a 'massacre'.[3]

Across India, tens of thousands of young Muslim men were forced to undergo sterilization under the government's controversial family planning programme aimed explicitly at controlling Muslim birth rate. Many Muslim leaders were arrested for speaking up against the Congress policies. Both the Turkman Gate atrocity and the brutal family planning operation were personally supervised by Indira Gandhi's

---

[3]Bose, Ajoy and Dayal, John. *For Reasons of State: Delhi Under Emergency*, Penguin Viking, 2018.

younger son, Sanjay Gandhi, who was later killed in a mysterious aeroplane crash.

The Muslim community had its revenge by voting en masse against the Congress party in the first post-Emergency elections held in 1977, leading to its first-ever defeat at the national level in independent India. The Congress party's Muslim vote bank dissolved overnight as the community threw its mighty electoral weight behind the newly formed Janata Party, a coalition of opposition parties that included the BJP. Some of the Congress party's traditional Muslim loyalists, notably the then influential Shahi Imam of Jama Masjid, Abdullah Bukhari, led the revolt against the party, in what marked the first public manifestation of the community's disenchantment with the Congress party. For the first time, Muslims openly started to question its 'secular' commitment to protect minorities, accusing it of paying merely lip service to get their votes. The Muslim–Congress relations never quite really recovered after that. Many Muslim leaders left the Congress party to join other new regional 'secular' parties such as the Janata Dal, Rashtriya Janata Dal (RJD) and the Samajwadi Party (SP).

But there was worse to come to damage its secular credentials in the eyes of minorities. The nationwide Sikh Massacre by the Congress cadres in 1984, instigated by its senior leaders, in retaliation against Indira Gandhi's assassination by her Sikh bodyguard, shattered whatever little faith minorities still had in the party's claim to be a secular guardian of their lives and liberties. Neither the 1977 anti-Muslim violence nor the 1984 Sikh massacre were aberrations, the fact being that the Congress party's record of protecting minorities and their interests has been disgraceful: there is a long history of violence against minorities, particularly Muslims, under the Congress party's rule. Radical Hindu groups might have instigated the violent incidents, but they happened under the Congress party's watch, and yet seldom were the perpetrators brought to book. The demolition of Babri Masjid on 6 December 1992, occurred under the Congress party's rule amid widespread criticism that then prime minister, P.V. Narasimha Rao, did nothing to prevent it. In *Half Lion: How P.V. Narasimha Rao Transformed India*, his biographer, Vinay Sitapati, denied conspiracy theories that Rao was involved in the plot, but in a media interview he acknowledged: 'However, there is no question that Rao prioritized personal and political ambition at one of the gravest moment's in India's post-independence history, and made a serious error of judgement in trying to negotiate with the Hindu right instead of imposing President's Rule in Uttar Pradesh.'[4] But the Congress party's role in the whole sordid Babri Masjid–Ram Mandir affair goes further back. Right back to Rajiv Gandhi, who, in

---

[4]Sharma, Betwa. 'Babri Masjid Demolition: Narasimha Rao Failed Muslims But So Did Congress, Says Former PM's Biographer', *HuffPost*, 2 December 2018, https://bit.ly/3C1CnyK. Accessed on 24 January 2022.

1986, as prime minister, ordered the locks of the Babri Masjid to be removed to allow Hindus to offer worship, thus reviving a dispute that had long gone into a deep freeze and paving the way for the Vishwa Hindu Parishad (VHP) to accelerate its Ram Janambhoomi movement to build a temple to the Hindu God, Ram, at the same spot where the mosque once stood.

So, why did he do it?

It was a classic Congress party move and its brand of secularism: an attempt to balance an act of Muslim appeasement with one of Hindu appeasement. Only a few days prior, acting under pressure from conservative Muslims, the Rajiv Gandhi government had brought in a law to overturn the Supreme Court's verdict in favour of an elderly divorced Muslim woman, Shah Bano, seeking monthly maintenance from her former husband, who had abandoned her to marry another woman without providing for her. The verdict sparked a Muslim backlash spearheaded by the fundamentalist All India Muslim Personal Law Board (AIMPLB), which called it an interference in the community's religious laws that govern matters relating to marriage and divorce. As protests spread, Gandhi capitulated, following it up barely weeks later with another act of capitulation—this time, to Hindu fundamentalists.

Arif Mohammad Khan, who was a minister in the Rajiv Gandhi government at the time but quit in protest against overturning the Supreme Court verdict, described the reopening of Babri Masjid's locks as a 'balancing act'. 'The announcement to reverse the SC judgement (Shah Bano case) and the removal of the locks happened within a span of two weeks. This to most people appeared as a balancing act and they hoped that now both the agitating parties would feel satisfied,' he told Indo-Asian News Service (IANS).[5] Former President Pranab Mukherjee described it as an 'error of judgment' by Rajiv Gandhi likening it to an act of 'absolute perfidy.[6]

Congress Secularism And Muslims

So much, then, for Congress party's secularism, and how the Hindu Right capitalized on it to feed its own agenda and created what must pass for one of the biggest myths of our times—namely, that secularism equals minorityism at the expense of the majority community's interests and concerns. Just a cursory glance at how the minorities fared during nearly five decades of the Congress party's complete monopoly of power will show how overcooked this myth actually is. Far from benefitting the minorities, it saw a steady institutionalization of anti-minority prejudice, especially directed at Muslims, allegedly the main beneficiaries of Congress party's incumbency.

---

[5]IANS, 'Unlocking of Babri Masjid Was a "Balancing Act" Post Shah Bano Case', *Business Standard*, 28 March 2017, https://bit.ly/3hJ5oGg. Accessed on 2 March 2022.
[6]Mukherjee, Pranab. *The Turbulent Years: 1980–1996*, Rupa Publications, New Delhi, 2016.

Widespread discrimination against Muslims in employment, housing and education, flourished under its watch as comprehensively documented by the Sachar Committee in its report in 2006 regarded as the most forensic investigation into the social, economic and educational condition of Muslims in India. The Committee headed by late Rajinder Sachar, former chief justice of Delhi High Court, was set up in 2005 by then prime minister, Dr Manmohan Singh to study the socio-economic status of Muslims.[7]

There is a long catalogue of abuse/misuse and flawed execution of secularism. There could be no bigger indictment of its failure than the fact that the very communities whose rights it was supposed to protect are now openly calling for it to be scrapped. The Muslim community, in particular, are so put off by it that probably it has more supporters among liberal Hindus than ordinary Muslims. The truth is that secularism never appealed to India's inherently conservative Muslims, who saw detaching religion from public life as un-Islamic. Islam doesn't recognize the notion of secular spaces and religion dominates all aspects of a good Muslim's daily life, beginning from when they get up in the morning until they go to bed at night. In Islam, a mosque is more than a mere place of worship; it's very much a public space

---

[7]Prime Minister's High-Level Committee For Preparation of Report on Social, Economic and Educational Status of the Muslim Community of India. *Social, Economic and Educational Status of the Muslim Community of India*, November 2006, https://bit.ly/3IPQqtV. Accessed on 3 March 2022.

around which daily life revolves.

To Indian Muslims, secularism's appeal was limited to the fact that it offered protection to their religious rights in a Hindu-majority country. As I have pointed out elsewhere, they would have been equally content with any other arrangement that offered them the same deal. And that remains their position today: they are not particularly hung up on what this arrangement is called so long as it allows them to preserve their Muslim identity and live with dignity and security. As Deng Xiaoping, who pioneered China's radical economic reforms, famously said, 'It doesn't matter whether a cat is white or black, as long as it catches mice.'[8] For the Muslims of India, the cat called secularism no longer catches mice, and they are ready to try one that might.

Unrealistic Expectation

An important point consistently ignored in the debate on Hindu–Muslim relations is that after the horrific events of Partition and the still-simmering bitterness over the long spell of Mughal rule in India, it was unrealistic to expect the two communities to live normally no matter how much you lowered the 'normality' threshold. World history is littered with cases of historically antagonistic communities not ever being able to co-exist normally. Take

---

[8]'Buckle, Mark. 'Black Cat, White Cat...', *China Daily*, 2 August 2018, https://bit.ly/3INYwmR. Accessed on 3 March 2022.

the Catholic–Protestant relations in Northern Ireland. One hundred years after Ireland's partition (1920) culminating in the declaration of independence in 1921 and 23 years after the 1998 Good Friday Agreement, aimed at ending sectarian violence in the region, relations between two communities remain extremely fraught with tensions always bubbling under the surface. Nobody even pretends that there's anything even approaching normality. Sinhalese–Tamil relations in Sri Lanka; continuing Tutsi–Hutu tensions in Rwanda, two decades after the end of the Rwandan civil war; Muslim–Christians in Lebanon; Turks and Kurds in Turkey; Shias–Sunnis across the Muslim world are just some of the other examples in this growing list.

Idealism and optimism may be noble instincts, but they are no match for realism. Yet, in different ways, both Nehru and Jinnah allowed their own liberalism (despite his regressive politics Jinnah, too, was a liberal at heart) to have the better of realism as they sought to impose their idealistic visions on their citizens. Unveiling his idea of Pakistan in his address to the Constituent Assembly of the newly minted nation on 11 August 1947, Jinnah spoke much in the same vein as Nehru did about his vision of modern India. The Pakistan of Jinnah's vision was to be inclusive, guaranteeing freedom of religion, the rule of law and equality for all irrespective of their religious, political and cultural affiliations. Urging the people to work together 'forgetting the past, burying the hatchet', he said:

> If you change your past and work together in a spirit that everyone of you, no matter to what community he belongs, no matter what relations he had with you in the past, no matter what is his colour, caste or creed, (he) is first, second, and last a citizen of this State with equal rights, privileges, and obligations there will be no end to the progress you will make...(and) in course of time Hindus would cease to be Hindus and Muslims would cease to be Muslims, not in the religious sense, because that is the personal faith of each individual, but in the political sense as citizens of the State.[9]

It is clear that Nehru in India and Jinnah in Pakistan were effectively trying to achieve the same end—creating modern liberal democracies where the faith of the individual would not matter, and everyone would be treated equally—but through different means: through secularism in India and faith-inspired communitarianism in Pakistan.

Eminent 'Partition' historians like the US-based Pakistani scholar Ayesha Jalal, whose 1985 book, *The Sole Spokesman*, is regarded as a seminal work on Jinnah, insist that he was unfairly portrayed as a sectarian bigot and that his demand for a separate Muslim nation had nothing do with religion. Yes, he used religion to mobilize Muslims, but his vision for Pakistan was not of an Islamic theocracy 'run by mullahs', but

---

[9]'Mr. Jinnah's Presidential Address to the Constituent Assembly of Pakistan', Pakistani.org, https://bit.ly/3I6NBU0. Accessed on 14 March 2022.

of a Muslim-majority country open to all as testified by his Constituent Assembly address.[10] But his premature death—within a year of the creation of Pakistan—changed the course of Pakistan's history. Jalal's view was broadly echoed by late BJP leader Jaswant Singh in his book *Jinnah: India, Partition, Independence*. Though Singh paid a heavy price for his defence of Jinnah as he was expelled by the BJP for compromising its 'ideology and discipline', the book succeeded in sparking a debate on the need for a new appraisal of Jinnah's role in Partition and his idea of Pakistan.[11]

The 'Ifs' of History

There is a popular counterfactual narrative that *if* Nehru and Jinnah had lived longer, they would not have allowed their dreams to wither away. In other words, things didn't go according to plan because they did not live long enough to see them through. But there's a more realistic explanation: there was a fundamental disconnect between their vision of western-style liberal democracy and what their people wanted. They simply took it upon themselves to decide what was good for their countryfolk and assumed that this was what the public wanted. But, as subsequent events showed, they were wrong. The problem was that people, neither in

---

[10]Jalal, Ayesha. *The Sole Spokesman: Jinnah, the Muslim League and the Demand for Pakistan*, Cambridge University Press, 1994.
[11]Singh, Jaswant. *Jinnah: India, Partition, Independence*, Rupa Publications, Delhi, 2009.

India, nor in Pakistan, were asked whether they agreed with their leaders' blueprint for the future. Let alone ordinary public, it is well-known that even within their own parties, neither Nehru nor Jinnah enjoyed unqualified support for their plans.

Constituent Assembly Debates

But let's stick to India. The debates in the Constituent Assembly on framing the Constitution (1946–50) revealed widely divergent views, and none other than Dr B.R. Ambedkar, its principal architect, led the opposition to prescribe a social and economic structure in the Constitution. Speaking on an amendment proposed by K.T. Shah (noted economist who was to later contest the first presidential election which he lost to Dr Rajendra Prasad) which sought to declare India a 'Secular, Federal, Socialist' nation, Ambedkar argued against imposing a future state policy framework on the people. The Constitution, he argued, was 'merely a mechanism for the purpose of regulating the work of the various organs of the State'.

In an impassioned intervention, he said:

> What should be the policy of the State, how the Society should be organised in its social and economic side are matters which must be decided by the people themselves according to time and circumstances. It cannot be laid down in the Constitution itself, because

that is destroying democracy altogether. If you state in the Constitution that the social organisation of the State shall take a particular form, you are, in my judgment, taking away the liberty of the people to decide what should be the social organisation in which they wish to live. It is perfectly possible today, for the majority people to hold that the socialist organisation of society is better than the capitalist organisation of society. But it would be perfectly possible for thinking people to devise some other form of social organisation which might be better than the socialist organisation of today or of tomorrow. I do not see therefore why the Constitution should tie down the people to live in a particular form and not leave it to the people themselves to decide it for themselves.[12]

Ambedkar put his finger at the heart of the issue: it would be wrong to impose any predetermined system of social and economic governance on the people without their consent. The fact that Shah's amendment failed to make it showed the strength of feeling on the issue in the Constituent Assembly. The words 'secularism' and 'socialism' were kept out of the Preamble to the Constitution until the controversial 42nd Amendment in 1976. One of the most contentious issues that Constitution makers faced was the

---

[12]Jha, Shefali. 'Secularism in the Constituent Assembly Debates, 1946-1950', *Economic and Political Weekly,* 27 July 2002, Vol. 37, No. 30, https://bit.ly/33Z4fXA. Accessed on 24 February 2022.

place of religion, and the religious rights of minorities in independent India. It dominated much of the three-year-long debate in the Constituent Assembly.

'When the preamble to the Constitution was discussed… disagreement and acrimonious debate over the incorporation of the principle of secularism took up most of the Assembly's time,' according to Prof. Shefali Jha of the Centre for Political Studies.[13]

While there was a broad agreement on the necessity of keeping the state secular, only because nobody wanted to be perceived as 'communal' for openly advocating a Hindu state, there were sharp differences over almost every aspect of how a secular state would function in a deeply religious society: whether secularism meant that the state strictly stayed out of religion altogether, or should it acknowledge religion as an irrefutable fact of Indian life but remain neutral while showing equal respect to all religions? There was a long debate on the exact scope of religious rights in a secular state, with many members opposed to a laissez-faire approach that would give citizens blanket freedom of 'religious worship' along with the right to profess, practise and propagate their faith publicly. They favoured a tighter and more limited definition with restrictions on practices or customs that were likely to be discriminatory or to undermine individual dignity—customs such as 'child marriage, polygamy, unequal

---

[13]Ibid.

laws of inheritance, prevention of inter-caste marriages, and dedication of girls to temples' in the name of religion.[14] There was also concern that minority rights should not be at the expense of the majority community.

Ultimately, however, the liberal view prevailed, and a version of secularism that Hindu groups saw as skewed in favour of minorities was adopted. This allegation gained wider currency in the following years because of the way it was used by the Congress party, and later, other self-proclaimed secular parties to build a Muslim constituency—obliging fundamentalist community leaders, as in the Shah Bano case and over *The Satanic Verses*, in exchange for help with Muslim votes and then 'balancing' this by obliging Hindu fundamentalists as in the Babri Masjid–Ram Mandir dispute. Secularism became a plaything in the hands of secularist politicians, and, ultimately, Muslims saw through it.

But there is another reason why they got disenchanted with it—the perception that secularism was against religion and people of faith. And this perception, cutting across the Hindu–Muslim divide, came about as a westernized, liberal, secular elite indulged in mocking the faithful and symbols of their religious identity as markers of religious

---

[14]Rao, B. Shiva. *The Framing of India's Constitution: Select Documents–Vol. II*, Government of India Press, Nasik, 1968, p. 72, cited in Jha, Shefali. 'Secularism in the Constituent Assembly Debates, 1946-1950', *Economic and Political Weekly*, 27 July 2002, Vol. 37, No. 30, https://bit.ly/33Z4fXA. Accessed on 24 February 2022

fundamentalism and cultural backwardness. This united most devout Indians, Hindus as well as Muslims, against what they saw as a common enemy. All of which brought us back to the challenge of creating a viable 'secular state in a religious society', as political scientist Prof. Shefali Jha noted in her commentary on the Constituent Assembly debates which showed that even many secularists, for all their enthusiasm, were nagged by anxiety: could a secular state survive in a society where there was no concept of a secular space and religion was everywhere?[15] It was an audacious enterprise powered by an idealistic belief that the pull of democracy and nationalism would ultimately supersede religious sectarianism. There was an expectation that once a secular state was established, its spirit would automatically percolate down the society, propelling it towards secularization over a period of time. A lot of hope was pinned, particularly, on the young generation of Indians, who, it was thought, would be able to transcend the hangover of Partition and the bitter history of Hindu–Muslim relations, which hobbled their parents and grandparents' generation. In the event, those expectations were belied.

The question now is: where do we go from here? Social and political scientist Prof. Neera Chandhoke said: 'Moments of crisis provide an opportunity to re-examine a concept, clarify what it means and stands for, what the

---

[15]Ibid.

political context of the concept is....(and) to reconsider the foundational presumptions of secularism...'[16] In other words, go back to the drawing board and start afresh, avoiding the mistakes of those who came before us.

But whatever course we finally choose (suitably tweak secularism to make it more acceptable and effective, or adopt a new system altogether, including a version of Hindu Rashtra) we must be guided by national mood and the new political realities. As the old adage goes: 'Those who forget the past are doomed to repeat it.' Beware.

---

[16]Chandhoke, Neera. 'Rethinking Secularism: A View From India', *global-e*, Vol. 10, No. 9, 14 February 2014, https://bit.ly/3HwI3Sq. Accessed on 24 February 2022.

4

Limits of Mass Action: The Shaheen Bagh Syndrome

'I love America more than any other country in the world and, exactly for this reason, I insist on the right to criticize her perpetually.'

—James Baldwin

No contemporary book on Hindu–Muslim relations would be complete without a mention of the Shaheen Bagh protest against the new citizenship law—the CAA—which is touted by many to be discriminatory against Muslims. Although, in retrospect, the CAA has failed, for the reasons I discuss later, its significance as the first major catalyst for the mobilization of the Muslim collective in independent India will remain. Two books on the Shaheen Bagh protests have already been published but unfortunately, both suffer from a lack of perspective and present a one-dimensional and hagiographic account of an event that requires—indeed, deserves—a more in-depth and rounded analysis.

A very important issue that has been overlooked is its implications for any future of Muslim direct action. Shaheen Bagh's failure amid politically fuelled conspiracy theories about its aims underlines the limits of any Muslim mass action not supported by the vast majority of the population; in other words, which is restricted to a minority group. For all the hype around it, the sad truth is that non-Muslim support for Shaheen Bagh protesters remained restricted mostly to the usual liberal suspects, and towards the end, even some of that support fizzled out. The most revealing was the reluctance of the so-called secular parties to be seen supporting a Muslim protest for fear of being seen as anti-Hindu.

Aam Aadmi Party's (AAP) Arvind Kejriwal, generally quick to seize any opportunity to burnish his claim to be a champion of democratic rights, carefully distanced himself from the protest, restricting his supposed opposition to the CAA to press statements. He refused to visit Shaheen

Bagh to engage with the protesters despite their repeated invitations to him.

Saba Rahman, a journalist, found it intriguing that a politician whose career was built on and around street protests became so coy when it came to showing solidarity with the Shaheen Bagh campaigners, going so far as to declare the protest a menace for the disruption to traffic on public route during a press conference. In an open letter to Kejriwal, she wrote that he, 'even avoided mentioning Shaheen Bagh in [his] rallies and interviews, even referring to the road blockade as a distraction'. She addressed the Delhi chief minister accusing him, 'mocking the home minister, you said you would have gotten the road vacated in two hours'.[1]

Political commentator Samir K. Purkayastha noted that for a 'self-proclaimed anarchist', like Kejriwal, his arm's-length approach to Shaheen Bagh was 'glaring'. 'Kejriwal, once termed infamously as protester-in-chief, is conspicuous by his absence from the scene of action,' he wrote on the digital news platform, *The Federal*.[2]

The Congress, too, didn't go beyond empty rhetoric—attacking the BJP but taking care not to be seen as being too cosy with Muslim protesters. The experience has left the community deeply demoralized and put paid to whatever

---

[1] Rahman, Saba. 'Mr Kejriwal, Delhi Is Done and Dusted, Shouldn't You Visit Shaheen Bagh Now?', *The Indian Express*, 14 February 2020, https://bit.ly/3HsQRc4. Accessed on 24 February 2022.

[2] Purkayastha, Samir K. 'Why is Kejriwal not taking a stand on Shaheen Bagh', *The Federal*, 30 January 2020, https://bit.ly/3sxfrEi. Accessed on 24 February 2022.

little enthusiasm it had for mass action. Let's revisit the protest at Shaheen Bagh, and on the way, examine what went wrong and what is likely to be its legacy.

By the way, there's no 'bagh' (garden) in Shaheen Bagh. And nothing 'shaheen' (majestic) about this lower- and middle-class Muslim ghetto sandwiched between the old settlements of Okhla and modern high-rise buildings of Sarita Vihar–Jasola Complex on the outskirts of South Delhi. Shaheen Bagh is a concrete jungle dotted with garbage dumps, open drains and stench-spewing nullahs. Home to an insecure, cowed minority community too scared to put its head above the parapet, it's hardly the sort of place you would expect to inspire revolutionary fervour. Insurrection and Shaheen Bagh?

So, its overnight rise to international fame as the site of a new 'Muslim awakening' surprised its own denizens. They said that they never imagined what was meant to be a token protest by a handful of women would grow into something so big and put their obscure slum on the world map. In just a few weeks following the passing of the CAA, Shaheen Bagh was transformed from a place few even knew existed into a symbol of countrywide Muslim resistance against the Act. Heaps of praises, bordering on romanticism, have been levied in speeches and writings about the courage and determination of the mostly uneducated, working-class women who led the protest. Stripped of the hype, however, Shaheen Bagh's significance was essentially two-fold.

Firstly, it was perhaps the first time in independent India

that the country's nearly 200 million Muslims had en masse coalesced around a non-denominational issue, in defence of India's constitutional values by using symbols of Indian nationalism to make their case. It was a historic departure for a community often much too preoccupied with its Islamic identity and more used to mobilizing around religious issues—sharia, Muslim Personal Law and triple talaq. Najeeb Jung, Delhi's former lieutenant governor, noted that the use of nationalist symbols (reciting the Preamble to the Constitution and singing the national anthem and 'Vande Matram') was 'a far cry from the time a Muslim MP [Member of Parliament] walked out of the Lok Sabha when the national song was being sung'.[3]

A second and related significance was that the protest was led by ordinary Muslims, mostly women. For once, mullahs were consciously kept at bay. Some Right-wing Muslim groups did attempt to infiltrate, but were quickly got rid of after a number of leading non-Muslim supporters of the Shaheen Bagh movement like the Congress party MP, Shashi Tharoor, expressed concern. From then on, no religious or communal discourse was allowed and organizers went to great lengths to ensure that it retained its broadly secular character. Writer and filmmaker Sohail Hashmi, in a conversation about the protests, told me:

---

[3]Jung, Najeeb. 'Capital Omen: Minorities in India Are Coming to Believe That There Is a Campaign to Make Them Second-Class Citizens', *The Indian Express*, 27 February 2020, https://bit.ly/3Iz0sPV. Accessed on 24 February 2022.

Shaheen Bagh was not mobilized or led by the 'Muslim Leadership'. The so-called 'Muslim leaders' were kept away. They tried their best to be seen there because they were afraid of being left behind, but failed to get into leadership positions. This was one of the most remarkable features of this agitation.

The protest might have failed to achieve its principal aim of getting the CAA withdrawn, but its ultimate triumph was that until the end, it managed to stay secular and inclusive. A joyful celebration of Indianness was its singular achievement, as rights activist Harsh Mander described. Mander, who visited Shaheen Bagh-style protest sites in 'every corner of the country', found them 'less protests... more celebrations of the reassurance that India still is equally their country...that we all stand together'. He was moved by the sight of 'men in skullcaps and women in hijabs joyfully waving the national flag shoulder to shoulder with Indians of other faiths'.[4]

How much of that spirit survives to inform Muslim outlook in future will be Shaheen Bagh's real legacy. Of course, it's easier said than done. It's important to remember that Shaheen Bagh was the product of a political and cultural climate of prejudice and intolerance, and for its spirit to survive, first, that climate must change; unless that happens

---

[4]Mander, Harsh. 'Protests Are Not Just Against the CAA-NRIC-NPR Trinity, but Have Already Succeeded in Numerous Ways', *The Indian Express*, 28 February 2020, https://bit.ly/3hvqRSN. Accessed on 24 February 2022.

it's hard to be overtly optimistic about the Shaheen Bagh's legacy. The fact that the protest ultimately withered away unsung and unlamented speaks for itself.

The Beginning

The story of the Shaheen Bagh movement began on a foggy winter afternoon—15 December 2019. But, as with all famous events, a number of myths and conspiracy theories came to surround the movement as its fame spread. Two myths, in particular, became a part of Shaheen Bagh folklore. So much so that many 'Shaheen Baghis' themselves began to believe them. The first is that the protest was started by women. It was, in fact, begun by a group of young male students led by Sharjeel Imam of Jawaharlal Nehru University (JNU) who was later arrested on charges of sedition due to a controversial speech he made at AMU. It began with a spontaneous dharna against a brutal police crackdown on students of Jamia Millia Islamia (JMI) University on the evening of 14 December 2019, following a violent incident at an anti-CAA protest near the campus. Cops stormed the university library, reportedly without the permission of JMI authorities, beat up students mercilessly and vandalized university property. Several students were injured and had to be hospitalized. As the news spread, the group led by Sharjeel Imam started blockading Kalindi Kunj Road, a busy highway bordering Shaheen Bagh. They ran the show for two days before women took over, encouraged by the female students from JMI whose colleagues had been victims of police action.

The second myth is that the protest was a 'spontaneous' response to Parliament passing the new citizenship law which explicitly excludes Muslims from a list of persecuted minorities in Pakistan, Bangladesh and Afghanistan, who would now be eligible for Indian citizenship. Together with a proposed National Population Register (NPR) and a National Register of Citizens (NRC), it is seen as a prelude to strip Muslims of their Indian citizenship if they are not able to produce documents required to prove their Indian roots. But the 'spontaneity' theory is not supported by the timeline: the law was adopted on 11 December, while Shaheen Bagh erupted on 15 December—four days later. In fact, the CAA became the focus of the protest only after the baton passed to women on 17–18 December. Until then, it was solely aimed at demanding action against policemen who were responsible for the JMI crackdown.

There were two reasons why Shaheen Bagh, rather than JMI, became the focal point. First, many of the students who were caught up in the police's attack were from Shaheen Bagh. The second was strategic: Shaheen Bagh was closest to a major highway and, therefore, considered an ideal place to stage a dharna, in order to attract public and media attention. Sure enough, within hours, the place was swarming with crews of major news media networks. Late that evening and for almost three months afterwards, Shaheen Bagh was to dominate media headlines.

The sheer novelty of hundreds of burkha-clad women, some with small children in tow, squatting in the middle of a busy road to assert their constitutional rights made for a good story. It was an image—at once, visually arresting and full of political significance—that came to define the movement prompting some commentators to hail it as marking the birth of a 'new Muslim woman'. As the movement gained momentum, it become a template for other anti-CAA campaigns spawning little 'Shaheen Baghs' across India—in Lucknow, Chennai, Bengaluru, Kolkata; Shaheen Bagh had become a brand.

Yet, when the protest began, few, even among its most optimistic supporters, expected it to last as long as it did. At most, they gave it a few weeks. The government, on its part, took a rather condescending approach—seeing it as an act of bravado that would fizzle out for lack of support. If that didn't happen, the protesters it reckoned would blink at the first sight of intimidation. It proved to be a gross misreading, not only of the determination of protesters, but also, more broadly, of the national mood marked by a simmering discontent among young people who had overwhelmingly voted for Prime Minister Narendra Modi on the back of his promise to give them jobs and opportunities for economic growth. They felt short-changed that the mandate they gave him was being used instead to push a divisive agenda they didn't wish to be a part of. According to an *India Today* poll in January 2020, they saw measures like the CAA as a diversion from the government's policy failures.[5] Shaheen Bagh, thus, became a lightning rod for accumulated angst over a range of issues—and, more importantly, across communities.

The agitation might have been started by Muslims, but soon it acquired an inclusive pan-India character, emerging as a symbol of secular solidarity against majoritarianism. Much like what happened in Hong Kong in 2019, when protests against a controversial extradition bill morphed into a wider platform in defence of democracy threatened by creeping authoritarianism. At its peak, Shaheen Bagh became the 'go-to' place for anyone remotely interested in politics—and, of course, a 'must' for foreign journalists.

Al Jazeera's Elizabeth Puranam wrote how when she came to India to cover the CAA controversy, she was told by friends that her first stop would have to be Shaheen Bagh: 'You have to go. You can't cover the protests without going there. The atmosphere is amazing. It's like a block party.' The day she visited was Delhi's 'coldest day in 100 years'.

> The temperature was dropping to as low as three degrees Celsius, but people—many of them women accompanied by their young children—sat on carpets on the road all day, while men stood on the sides.

---

[5]'Most Indians Say CAA, NRC Are Attempts to Divert Attention From Unemployment: MOTN Poll', *India Today*, 23 January 2020, https://bit.ly/3HHhx8V. Accessed on 2 March 2022.

Protesters listened to speakers talk about secularism and the constitution, and how the Modi government was threatening to undermine both.[6]

She was struck by the 'jovial atmosphere' and mood of solidarity among the participants. 'A young man passed a large cardboard box full of hot samosas around. A student distributed boxes of vegetable biryani; others handed out bananas and bottled water.'[7]

Stories about Shaheen Bagh's famed hospitality—complimentary tea, biscuits, biryani, endless mithai—became the talk of the town, though, alas, I missed out on them every time I visited. Shaheen Bagh's critics, principally, the BJP, seized on these reports to float conspiracy theories that the protest was bankrolled by shadowy foreign sources. It was a 'plot', they alleged, to discredit Narendra Modi and destabilize India.

'What's happening in Shaheen Bagh in the name of opposing CAA is an Islamist insurrection', tweeted Amit Malviya, BJP spokesman and the head of its IT cell. The party also alleged that women were paid to sit on dharna. It put out a video in which an unnamed man (his face hidden from the camera) claimed that the payment ranged from ₹500 to ₹1,200 for a 'shift'. A senior Delhi BJP

---

[6] Puranam, Elizabeth. 'Why Shaheen Bagh Protests Are an Important Moment in India's History', *Al Jazeera*, 3 February 2020, https://bit.ly/3HCTojQ. Accessed on 24 February 2022.
[7] Ibid.

leader, Vijay Jolly, called them 'bikau' (saleable commodity). No evidence was produced by independent fact-checking organizations to back these allegations.

The protest's organizers insisted it was funded with voluntary donations, mostly in kind. Local Muslim shopkeepers and restaurant-owners sent food; someone offered to pay for tents; someone else helped out with public address system.

'*Yeh sab bhai-chaare per chal raha hai* [It's all running on mutual cooperation],' Mohammed Sayeed, a volunteer told me. He ran a grocery store and was happy to donate whatever he could to the cause. 'Milk, tea bags, sugar...whatever they need. *In ki ladai hamari ladai hai* [Their struggle is our struggle],' he said. A group of visiting Sikh farmers organized a massive 'langar' to feed the activists, while volunteers of Khidmat Foundation, a social welfare collective, served tea and refreshments. A group distributed 'secular chai' under a banner that read: 'Secular Chai—Made in India'.

Accounts of gratis biryani, I was repeatedly told, were vastly exaggerated and part of BJP's propaganda to undermine the protest. Yes, it was occasionally distributed. But only when someone brought it on a special occasion. '*Kabhi, kabhi koi de jaata hai* [Occasionally, someone brings it to the protest],' Sangeeta, a student volunteer from JMI, said, hastening to clarify that she herself was a vegetarian and had no interest in biryani.

The biryani tag, however, stuck, even spawning some off-colour jokes. But in the bitter culture wars over the CAA this was small beer compared with more serious attempts to undermine the Shaheen Bagh campaign. It was accused of 'indoctrination'. The BJP circulated a video purporting to show how Muslim parents were using little children as 'propaganda tools' in their 'hate' campaign against prime minister Modi. It showed a small girl saying that Muslims would take 'revenge' against those who are 'attacking us'. The video also claimed that children were being encouraged to raise inflammatory slogans such as demanding *'Jinnah ki Azadi'*, and abusing Modi. 'Shocking! In the name of protests, depraved minds are exploiting the innocence of young kids, especially girls, for their propaganda and stirring animosity... We have seen this kind of indoctrination among kids in radical Islamic societies. But in #ShaheenBagh?', said Amit Malviya in a tweet accompanying the video.[8]

Even as the video's veracity remained in doubt, TV channels went to town, echoing its claim with sensational headlines. As culture wars intensified, some children from Shaheen Bagh reported that they were being called 'Pakistani' by their schoolmates. It's true that there were children on the site, but mostly infants wrapped up in their mothers' arms or sitting in their laps, blissfully unaware of what was going around them. The older ones mucked around, occasionally joining in slogan chanting. Women who brought their

---

[8] @amitmalviya. Twitter, 17 January 2020, 2.07 p.m., https://bit.ly/35Ie8JF. Accessed on 28 February 2022.

children along argued that they did so only because there was nobody to look after them at home. There was, however, some criticism, even among supporters, when a four-month-old child, Mohammad Jahan, who was taken to the protest site by his parents almost every day, died of severe cold and congestion on 30 January.[9] The Supreme Court weighed in after a 12-year-old National Bravery Award winner Zen Gunratan Sadavarte wrote to the Chief Justice S.A. Bobde seeking probe into the infant's death and calling for a ban on taking children to the dharna site.

'Can a four-month-old child go for the protest?' he asked as a Bench headed by him issued notices to the central and Delhi governments on the issue. The dead child's mother, Nazia, remained firm that she would continue protesting along with her two surviving children (a one-year-old boy and a five-year-old girl) as the new citizenship law was the reason for her child's death.

Tactical Errors

Controversy dogged the Shaheen Bagh protests throughout its short-lived resistance, with some of its own tactical errors feeding into the Hindu Right's propaganda war against it. First, there was an attempt to impose a Muslim/Islamic

---

[9]Vaidyanathan, A. "'4-Month-Old Goes for Protest?" Top Court Fumes Over Shaheen Bagh Death', NDTV, 10 February 2020, https://bit.ly/3IMRMW8. Accessed on 3 March 2022.

identity by chanting 'Allahu Akbar' and flaunting religious symbols, which drew criticism from some of its prominent non-Muslim allies who felt that bringing religiosity into a campaign, ostensibly in defence of secularism and inclusion, was against its spirit. Many liberal Muslims too felt uncomfortable. Its critics, of course, were quick to seize on it to claim that they had been right to portray it as a Muslim 'plot'. Slogans calling for 'azadi' (freedom) also handed ammunition to Right-wing Hindu nationalists who accused the protesters of echoing Kashmiri separatists and speaking the 'language of Imran Khan'.[10] The BJP argued that it was akin to Jinnah's separatist call for freedom from India. Then, one of the architects of the Shaheen Bagh campaign, Sharjeel Imam, was arrested and thrown in jail on charges of sedition for allegedly making inflammatory speeches against the CAA and the planned NRC.

But the harshest criticism that Shaheen Bagh faced was over the decision to continue the protest even after it became apparent that it had hit a dead end. Crucially, after the Delhi State Assembly elections in February, it lost its political cachet, easing the pressure on the government to reach out to the protesters. It also ceased to be of any use to the opposition parties, which had once courted them to embarrass the government. Even before the elections,

---

[10]Shali, Pooja, and Singh, Ram Kinkar. 'Arvind Kejriwal, Rahul Gandhi Speak Same Language As Imran Khan: Amit Shah', *India Today*, 24 January 2020, https://bit.ly/3C6Exgt. Accessed on 28 February 2022.

organizers were under pressure to review their tactics amid concern that it was becoming a lightning rod for the BJP and its affiliates to polarize opinion on religious lines ahead of the elections. Home Minister Amit Shah, told voters at an election rally to 'press the button so hard that the current reaches Shaheen Bagh'.[11] This, after another minister, Anurag Thakur, speaking at a rally and alluding to anti-CAA protesters, encouraged the crowd to call for the 'traitors' ('*saale gaddar*') to be shot.[12] His fellow party MP, Parvesh Varma, described the protesters as 'Muslims who want to take over India'. If Shaheen Bagh was allowed to continue it would create a 'Kashmir-like situation...and they will enter homes and rape (our) sisters and daughters'.[13] Quick on the heels of these statements, there were two incidents of firing. In one, a man opened fire at protesters in Shaheen Bagh, saying: 'This country is not for everyone. It's only for Hindus.'[14] A few days earlier, a gunman had fired at an anti-CAA march near JMI, injuring a student's arm.

---

[11]"The Wire Bulletin | "Press the Lotus Button So Hard That Shaheen Bagh Feels The Current": Amit Shah', YouTube, 27 January 2020, https://bit.ly/35GuYJC. Accessed on 10 March 2022.

[12]'Watch: Union minister Anurag Thakur leads "goli maaro saalon ko" slogans at rally', *Scroll.in*, 27 January 2020, https://bit.ly/3MGpP4B. Accessed on 11 March 2022.

[13]Pandey, Neelam. 'BJP MP says Shaheen Bagh protesters will "rape, kill" as party makes it Delhi poll plank', *The Print*, 28 January 2020, https://bit.ly/3KDIYm9. Accessed on 11 March 2022.

[14]Shukla, Saurabh. 'Firing At Shaheen Bagh, Delhi's Second In 3 Days At An Anti-CAA Protest', NDTV, 1 February 2020, https://bit.ly/3HNw96S. Accessed on 2 March 2022.

It was clear that Shaheen Bagh was being used for questionable political purposes. Many of its key supporters, including left-liberal groups like Sahmat, ANHAD (Act Now for Harmony and Democracy) and Karavan-e-Mohabbat, reportedly conveyed their concerns and suggested a pause. When their advice was rejected, they started to distance themselves; and after the post-election communal riots in Northeast Delhi, withdrew completely. The riots were seen as a culmination of the CAA-related tensions, and some believed that these tensions could perhaps have been defused by suspending the protest. That could have deprived its detractors of the pretext to use it to whip up religious passions in the run-up to the elections.

A few days after the riots, on 27 February 2020, a group of prominent rights activists led by Harsh Mander (Karavan-e-Mohabbat), Shabnam Hashmi (ANHAD), Apoorvanand and Syeda Hameed issued a public appeal to Shaheen Bagh protesters to withdraw their agitation 'in light of the violence and death, and as a mark of respect towards the dead and injured'.[15]

'This is for the courageous women protesters to ultimately decide. But we are convinced that the task of the moment should be to provide solace to the afflicted, calm nerves of the society and establish peace. We cannot afford the loss

---

[15] Apoorvanand. 'The Light of Shaheen Bagh', Seema Mustafa (ed.), *Shaheen Bagh and the Idea of India: Writings on a Movement for Justice, Liberty and Equality*, Speaking Tiger Books, New Delhi, 2020, p. 253–54.

of a single more innocent life,' they said, adding, 'When we see violence unleashed under the excuse of opposing these protests, we want to say that first and foremost we stand for peace.'[16]

Addressing fears that the disengagement would be seen as a sign of defeat, they said:

> This withdrawal won't be defeat in any way. It is a retreat in the best Gandhian tradition which valued human lives most. The movement in future weeks and months must focus on the one hand on preventing the NPR, and on the other to further strengthen unity, love and solidarity between Hindus, Muslims, Sikhs, Christians, and indeed people of every faith, and non-believers. We appeal to all the protesters to get involved in relief, healing and peace-making work, along with resisting NPR.[17]

The signatories—all ardent supporters of the Shaheen Bagh protest—stressed that they continued to back the anti-CAA campaign, but believed that the post-riots situation needed a different and more delicate response. They were disappointed when their appeal was not acquiesced to, upon which, they effectively dissociated themselves from Shaheen Bagh to focus on providing relief to those affected by the riots. They were, in turn, accused by some in the Shaheen

---

[16]Ibid.
[17]Ibid.

Bagh campaign of telling people in riot-hit areas that they were 'victims of Shaheen Bagh'.

Mohammed Fahim, a PhD scholar from AMU, who set up a library at Shaheen Bagh protest site and was actively involved in the campaign, told me: 'The narrative there is that we in Shaheen Bagh were responsible for their plight.' While he rejected that view, he said: 'I can see where they are coming from.'

The protest also faced a public backlash—much of it, politically-inspired—over the prolonged closure of a busy highway connecting three states—Delhi, Uttar Pradesh and Haryana—and used by thousands of commuters every day. The closure led to long delays and traffic snarls; and a shutdown of many local businesses. Protesters acknowledged the inconvenience the sit-in was causing but insisted that the cause they were fighting for was more important. '*Hum apne wajood ke liye ladd rahen hain* [We are fighting for our existence]', Salima Begum, a nursery school teacher, told me pointing out that she had given up her own part-time job at a local school to join the protest.

Fuaad Ahmed, a computer engineer, told me that his computer and mobile repair shop was among those shut down because of the occupation of the Shaheen Bagh area by the protesters, but he didn't mind. '*Kabhi, Kabhi* personal sacrifice *karna padta hai* [Sometime you have to make personal sacrifices].'

Protesters remained defiant even after an intervention

by the Supreme Court. Following a public interest litigation (PIL) plea filed by advocate and activist, Amit Sahni, and a BJP leader, Nand Kishore Garg, seeking removal of the protest on the grounds that it had disrupted daily life in the area, two interlocutors—senior advocates Sanjay Hegde and Sadhana Ramachandran—were appointed by to persuade the protesters to shift the sit-in. Incidentally, both were Shaheen Bagh sympathizers but were snubbed and returned empty-handed. Sanjay Hegde, rubbishing the rampant conspiracy theories, told a TV channel he had sent packets of sweets and cookies.

The End

Ultimately, it was COVID-19 that brought the protest in Shaheen Bagh to an end. On the morning of 24 March, exactly 100 days after it began, Delhi Police moved in and forcibly removed the protesters; pulled down the famous red tent that had been a home to them for more than three months and had become a symbol of 'Muslim resistance'; dismantled the various facilities; and cleared the road that had been blocked since December 2019. 'We saw history being demolished right in front of our eyes,' said Yaqoob, a student volunteer. Today, people driving past Shaheen Bagh wouldn't know that it was once the site of one of independent India's most talked-about public protesters.

In the end, it was a tame denouement as the authorities

seized the COVID-19 pandemic as a convenient justification to forcibly shut down the protest. Protesters offered little resistance, sticking to the non-violent spirit of the protest. It took the police just under an hour to finish the job, bringing to an end to one of the most emotive grassroots movements India has seen in recent memory.

Eyewitnesses recounted that the mood among the protesters was one of sullen defiance as the police tried to evict them; they were keen to register their protest but without provoking a confrontation. As they slowly left the site, they insisted it was not the end of their campaign, but only a 'pause' imposed by an 'undemocratic' government.

'The protest will continue. We will first fight novel coronavirus and then come back to defeat hateful and divisive politics,' Hena Ahmad, a protestor, told reporters as she watched the iconic tent being pulled down. Shaheen Bagh, according to her, was a 'thought process', and it couldn't be destroyed by simply physically removing the protesters from the site. Ritu Kaushik, who had been at the forefront of the resistance, accused the government of using COVID-19 to force the protesters to end their demonstration. She said: 'Delhi Police came to the spot at a time when the case of the road was still in Supreme Court. They removed not just the tent, but the library, posters, everything. It was evident that the government was not only fighting COVID-19 but also the Shaheen Bagh protest.'[18]

Delhi Police claimed that they had acted to enforce the official ban on public gatherings following a countrywide lockdown to pre-empt the spread of COVID-19. They were forced to move in after their appeal to the protesters to disperse failed.

'We had requested the protesters to leave in the morning due to the coronavirus outbreak and the lockdown that has been imposed. They refused and action was taken. Violators have been detained and the site has been cleared,' said R.P. Meena, deputy commissioner of police for the area.[19]

The public reaction was muted, to put it mildly. Most, including Shaheen Bagh's supporters who were concerned about the protesters' health, quietly welcomed it. Ultimately, Shaheen Bagh was undone by its own tactical miscalculations. However, until the push predictably came to a shove and the police moved in to enforce the countrywide lockdown to contain the spread of COVID-19, protesters had maintained that they were not going anywhere even if it meant exposing themselves to the deadly virus. They would rather have succumbed to the virus than 'surrender'.

Hume beemari se dar nahin hai, hume Modi ke kaale kanoon se dar hai [We are not scared of virus, we're scared

---

[18] Ajmal, Anam. 'How Delhi Cops End 100-Day Shaheen Bagh Protest', *The Times of India*, 25 March 2020, https://bit.ly/37cm3Qx. Accessed 2 March 2022.

[19] Lakhani, Somya. 'Shaheen Bagh sit-in protest cleared amid coronavirus lockdown', *The Times of India*, 24 March 2020, https://bit.ly/35OupNn. Accessed on 2 March 2022.

of Modi's black law],' said Gulnar Bibi, echoing the refrain: *'Shaheen Bagh protest nahin band hoga jab tak CAA nahin wapas liye jaayega* [The protest will not be lifted unless CAA is withdrawn].'

The only concession was to cap the numbers so that no more than 50 protesters were allowed to join the sit-in at a given time. But the scaling-down meant that the protest lost whatever little steam it had managed to retain. Effectively abandoned (an expression used by protesters themselves) by many of its erstwhile allies; frowned upon by courts (first by Delhi High Court, later by Supreme Court); pushed off the front pages by the COVID-19 story; and forced to cap the numbers, by March, Shaheen Bagh had gone into irreversible decline. Funds had dried up (forget biryani, even tea was hard to get); the generosity of local suppliers had run its course; and crowdfunding efforts were flagging. All of this, inevitably, was starting to take its toll on the protesters' morale, fighting talk notwithstanding. A well-known graphic novelist, Vishwajyoti Ghosh, whom I met at Shaheen Bagh just days before the police crackdown, was puzzled why they were persisting with it. 'I thought coronavirus [sic] scare would have been a good face-saver to withdraw.' The flexibility to adapt and change tactics when the situation changes is the hallmark of a good strategy.

Throughout the long agitation, tactics remained a mystery to most observers. Even when there were occasions that offered them a chance to find an honourable way out, they refused to take them allowing emotions to override hard-headed pragmatism, and, in the process, inadvertently helping their detractors. Instead, Shaheen Bagh got bogged down in a 'no-exit' strategy.

There was concern in liberal circles that the movement had got stuck in a conceptual and strategic cul-de-sac. Its outreach had remained confined to the Muslim constituency. It needed to broaden its aims and develop a new strategic framework to achieve those aims.

'The protests have achieved considerable normative success; but without a change of tack, it is difficult to see this translate into political victory, because the constituency of supporters remains limited, the government adamant, and countervailing institutional forces ambivalent. There are indications too of counter-mobilisation and consolidation,' argued Ruchi Gupta, the joint secretary of the All India Congress Committee.[20]

The question that Shaheen Bagh faced was whether it wanted to remain a single-issue, single-constituency or evolve into a wider political movement. According to Pushparaj Deshpande of Samruddha Bharat Foundation, a liberal Delhi-based think-tank, the movement needed to be diversified and taken beyond the confines of Muslim-CAA controversy to build a broader grassroots campaign by involving other marginalized groups such as the Dalits,

---

[20]Gupta, Ruchi. 'The Anti-CAA Protests Have Hit a Wall. Here Is Why', *Hindustan Times*, 13 February 2020, https://bit.ly/3Klc3T1. Accessed on 2 March 2022.

Adivasis and women threatened by the politics of exclusion and majoritarianism. 'Shaheen Bagh protest faces both organisational and psychological fatigue. It is important to take stock and build more sustainable linkages across interest groups. If progressives are genuinely committed to safeguarding and furthering the constitutional idea of India, it is imperative that this movement be immediately diversified,' he said.[21]

It was possible to diversify without necessarily losing the spirit of the Shaheen Bagh phenomenon. In fact, its inclusive spirit and 'vitality' were an asset that would make diversification easy; he said, 'Progressives must continue replicating the vitality of Shaheen Bagh in newer places.'

Saloni Kumar, a JNU scholar who had been associated with Shaheen Bagh since 'day one', told me that she was sad to see it 'go to seed'. 'I have been a witness to both its dramatic rise and precipitous declines, which saddens me. Because it was not meant to end like this,' she said.

So, what happened?

She reckoned that it became a victim of its own initial success. Organizers were 'mesmerised' by all the media attention and the celebrity endorsement leading them to believe they had already won the battle and all they needed to win the war was just to keep at it.

---

[21]Deshpande, Pushparaj. 'The Future of Progressive Politics in India', *Economic and Political Weekly*, Vol. 55, No. 14, 4 April 2020, https://bit.ly/3IMxtbt. Accessed on 2 March 2022.

'Remember, these were people who had no previous experience of a mass movement. It was an entirely new experience for them. I know women who had not stepped out of their homes before and were now giving sound bites to TV reporter. They found all this very exhilarating and empowering, and got carried away by the hype. I doubt they even noticed when things started to go wrong,' Ms Kumar said.

She said that she was involved in discussions to rethink the strategy when it looked like it had become stagnant and was benefiting the BJP. 'It was very frustrating. I remember I was told that if I was not happy I was free to go.' I heard similar stories from others. And several activists actually left in a huff after being snubbed. In the words of one veteran Left-wing campaigner, popularly known as 'Comrade': 'It felt like the revolution had started to eat its own children'. He stayed on to fight but was increasingly marginalized. Last time I met him, he told me that he had been reduced to making public safety announcements.

'Comrade' pointed out that in taking an inflexible stand, and continuing their agitation in the same form 'come what may' until the CAA was withdrawn, the protesters backed themselves into a corner. They also appeared to overlook one important fact, namely, that while the government could afford to sit out a long war of attrition, the protesters couldn't. They also ignored another factor: the logistics of keeping an open-ended operation on the road indefinitely. Comrade continued:

> Let me clarify that there was never any doubt about the legitimacy of the cause which remained popular. The criticism was that it was not working in its present form, and that we needed a pause while we worked on an alternative form of continuing it. But the organisers were concerned that [if] it was withdrawn it might lose momentum. There was also the argument that the government would interpret it as a defeat of the movement.

For the sake of perspective, it's important to point out that Shaheen Bagh was almost universally acknowledged even by its critics (outside the Sangh Parivar) as a profound moment for the Muslim community. It gave a new life to a demoralized community, which had gone into a shell in the aftermath of the Babri Masjid demolition, and the daily humiliations it suffered under the Modi government.

'For the first time in recent memory, these protests are making Indians acutely aware of the historic moment India is in', said Pushparaj Deshpande even as he questioned its methods.[22]

Lessons for the Government

But if the protesters' tactics appeared odd, the government's strategy of demonizing Shaheen Bagh and the Muslim

---

[22]Ibid.

community as 'Islamist insurrectionists', 'gaddaar' (traitors), and the voice of India's enemies was even odder. A refusal to negotiate was one thing, but to denounce people as seditious thugs for simply exercising their democratic right to protest against what they regarded as an unjust law, looked like a deliberate attempt to humiliate Muslims. Moreover, it flew in the face of Modi's election pledge that he would listen to everyone and carry everyone with him. He promised 'Sab ka saath, sab ka vikas [Everyone's support, everyone's development].' Yet, his attitude towards anti-CAA protestors conveyed exactly the opposite message. Muslims felt that they were dealt a double whammy: first, a law that discriminated against them on the basis of religion; or at least this was how it appeared to them, and then, a systematic campaign to demonize them as fifth columnists—'*saale gaddar* [bloody traitors]', who deserved to be 'shot dead' ('*goli maaro*'). The party failed to take any action against those who made such remarks encouraging others to indulge in similar incendiary rhetoric. The Muslim community could be forgiven for thinking that such attacks had the covert support of the leadership.

The problem with this strategy was that it had the effect of further alienating a community already feeling under siege. It fuelled the sense, even among moderate Muslims, that since the Modi government came to power six years ago, they had been deliberately targeted as part of a push towards the RSS's idea of a Hindu India. It was also a dangerous strategy from the point of view of national security. Let's not forget that both domestic and foreign radical Islamist groups are circling around, waiting to pounce. So far, Indian Muslims have managed to escape their clutches, but the longer they feel under pressure and that they are being relegated to second-class citizens in an increasingly 'Hindu India', the more vulnerable they're likely to become to radicalization.

Since the Babri Masjid was demolished, an entire generation of Muslims has grown up in a climate of anti-Muslim rhetoric and prejudice; and there is a gnawing fear that they may not prove as resilient as their parents' generation. I have heard Muslim parents worry about the effect of the prevailing state-sponsored Islamophobia on impressionable young Muslims. Statements such as the AMU student leader Faizul Hasan's intemperate outburst that Muslims have exhausted their 'limits of patience', and the inflammatory remarks of the AIMIM MLA, Akbaruddin Owaisi, may have been made in the heat of the moment, but they reflect the intense sense of frustration in the community. It will be a mistake to shrug them off as the rants of fringe elements.

This is a mistake the liberal class made in relation to Right-wing Hindu groups in the early days of Hindutva. Their actions and utterances were dismissed as the ramblings of a 'lunatic fringe'. It didn't take long for this 'lunatic fringe' to become the mainstream of Sangh Parivar. Many of the once-fringe figures are today in positions of power, most notably, Yogi Adityanath, chief minister of Uttar Pradesh. Of all the BJP chief ministers, he took the hardest line against CAA protesters, cracking down particularly heavily against the Shaheen Bagh-style sit-in in Lucknow.

If one were in Modi's shoes, one would tread very cautiously in pushing the 'Hindu India' project since it may be helping Muslim radicalization and potentially jeopardizing national security. Six years of relentless Muslim-baiting has taken a heavy toll on the community's capacity to resist fundamentalist tendencies and left it more exposed to radical influence. Particularly vulnerable is the new generation of Muslims growing up in a palpably hostile climate. They could prove easy pickings for Islamist groups looking for new recruits in the subcontinent. It's a risk the government cannot afford to shrug off.

It's imperative that an approach that risks radicalizing an otherwise-moderate community is discouraged. The best way to avert another Shaheen Bagh is to reach out to Muslims, or to, at least, avoid alienating them further. The prospect of India—a country with a proud tradition of inclusion and pluralism—being lumped with the countries it accuses of persecuting their minorities (the avowed rationale for CAA) should fill every patriotic Indian with horror.

5

Hostage to Religious Nationalisms

*'Muslims are a part of India. This is a fact of history...
We cannot imagine an India without Muslims.'*

—Satyajit Ray, *Ghare Baire*

In Europe, every schoolchild grows up having learnt about the horrors of European nationalism and how it led to the rise of fascism and emergence of Adolf Hitler. From an early age, they learn to be wary of hyper-nationalism, particularly that inspired by religious sectarianism and racial prejudice. In contrast, in India and

Pakistan, schoolchildren grow up learning only the glories of nationalism, and stories of their respective nationalist heroes. (We often confuse nationalism, an intrinsically exclusionist sentiment, with patriotism which is an essentially inclusive phenomenon.) Thus, the role of competing Hindu and Muslim nationalisms in causing Partition is seldom, if at all, dispassionately discussed, in either India or Pakistan, except to blame it all on the other side. Consequently, young people in these countries grow up blissfully unaware of the hazards of nationalism motivated by sectarian considerations which makes them vulnerable to repeating the mistakes of their ancestors.

Historically, rival Hindu–Muslim nationalisms have been the single most important factor in damaging community relations. The row over the new citizenship law that spawned the Shaheen Bagh protest was also rooted in the culture clash which has historically shaped Hindu–Muslim relations. Although the protest has ended, the debate continues—marked, on both sides, by selective interpretations of speeches and writings of leading Hindu and Muslim nationalists. The most prominent literature in the discourse includes Hindu Mahasabha leader, V.D. Savarkar's philosophy of Hindutva, and the Muslim League president, Mohammed Ali Jinnah's two-nation theory that lay behind the creation of Pakistan.

The Two-Nation Theory

My enduring image of the Shaheen Bagh protest is of Mohammed Abid, a software engineer, sitting in front of a replica of India Gate on the protest site and seemingly lost in reading the RSS ideologue, M.S. Golwalkar's treatise on Hindu identity and nationality, *We, or Our Nationhood Defined*. Published in 1939, it is regarded as one of the seminal texts on Hindu nationalism and has been dubbed the desi equivalent of Adolf Hitler's *Mein Kampf* in its take on ethnic minorities. Abid insisted on reading out to me a passage he had heavily underlined in red, which, he said, encapsulated the essence of the CAA. It was the much-cited and debated passage in which Golwalkar controversially defined only Hindus as Indians. He wrote that Muslims and non-Hindus could be regarded as Indians only if they relinquished their own religious and cultural practices and beliefs, and wholly embraced Hinduism. Alternative, they could live in India as only second-class citizens.

Abid was livid: 'This is what is behind CAA. It's all part of the RSS's Hindu Rashtra agenda. *Sab saaf, saaf nazar aa raha hai* [Everything is becoming clear].'

In the wake of the CAA, many Muslims like Abid are trying to catch up with the history of Right-wing Hindu nationalism. And they still have a lot of catching up to do. The CAA may not exactly be a prelude to the aspirations of RSS-inspired nationalists to create a Hindu Rashtra, but it clearly has a majoritarian edge that is rooted in, and reinforces the idea of the Muslim as an 'outsider'. It's not an innocent piece of legislation, but has deep ideological roots going back to the 1930s—the glory days of the now-defunct Hindu Mahasabha, which, under then president, Savarkar, espoused the 'two-nation' theory that saw Hindus and Muslims as two culturally separate nations—a theory that Jinnah was to borrow later to justify his campaign for a separate 'Muslim nation'.

The passage in Golwalkar's book that so offended Abid was, in fact, a recycled version of the theory originally propounded by Savarkar, who is considered the intellectual father of Hindu nationalism. Golwalkar's work was an abridged translation of Savarkar's 1934 Marathi language book, *Rashtra Mimansa* (*Nationalism*). It is relevant to point out that, like the minds behind the CAA, Savarkar considered Sikhism, Jainism and Buddhism as part of the Hindu parivar (family) while Muslims were excluded from his vision of Indianness. He stressed social and community unity between Hindus, Sikhs, Buddhists and Jains, to the exclusion of Muslims and Christians.

He argued that since the holiest sites of Islam and Christianity lay in the Middle East and not on the India subcontinent, the loyalties of Muslims and Christians to India and the homeland were divided. They were 'misfits' in the Indian civilization and could not truly be regarded as a part of the nation.[1] In the booklet, *Hindutva*, published in 1923, Savarkar explained that only Hindus could lay claim to being an Indian. He wrote:

> ...in the case of our Mohammedan or Christian countrymen who had originally been forcibly converted to a non-Hindu religion... are not and cannot be recognised as Hindus. For though Hindustan to them is Fatherland as to any other Hindu, yet it is not to them a Holy land too. Their holy land is far off in Arabia or Palestine. Their mythology and godmen, ideas and heroes are not the children of this soil. Consequently, their names and their outlook smack of a foreign origin. Their love is divided.

Savarkar made no secret of the fact that he was influenced by European fascism, particularly the Nazi ideology of a 'pure' German race, not 'contaminated' by 'outsiders'. He criticized Nehru for opposing Nazism, arguing, 'Surely, Hitler knows better than Pandit Nehru does what suits Germany best.'[2] In his book, *Hindu Rashtra Darshan* (1949) Savarkar wrote, 'Nazism proved undeniably the saviour of Germany.'[3] He

---

[1] Clarke, Sathianathan. *Competing Fundamentalisms: Violent Extremism in Christianity, Islam, and Hinduism*, Westminster John Knox Press, 2017.
[2] Casolari, Marzia. 'Hindutva's Foreign Tie-up in the 1930s', *Economic and Political Weekly*, Vol. 35, No. 4, 22 January 2000, https://bit.ly/35uZyFY. Accessed on 2 March 2022.
[3] 'Hindu Rashtra Darshan', Bhartiya Janata Party Central Library, https://bit.ly/3hZW5BU. Accessed on 11 March 2022.

drew parallels between the German majority and Jewish minority in Germany, and the Hindu majority and Muslim minority in India—criticizing both German Jews and Indian Muslims for supposedly failing to assimilate with majority beliefs.

In 1938, he warned, 'But if we Hindus in India grow stronger in time, these Moslem friends of the [Muslim] league type will have to play the part of German Jews.'[4]

Savarkar endorsed the idea of India as a Hindu Rashtra which became the basis of the 'two-nation' theory espoused by the Hindu Mahasabha, and later, the RSS, led by Golwalkar for more than 30 years. Golwalkar's most explicit elucidation of the idea of 'Hindu India' came in his essay, 'Our Identity and Nationality', which later appeared in a collection of his writings, *Guruji: Vision and Mission*. It read:

> All the elements required to develop as a great nation are present in this Hindu society in their entirety. This is why we say that in this nation of Bharat, living principles of the Hindu society are the living systems of this nation. In short, this is 'Hindu Nation.'[5]

It is clear that any attempt to deny a link between the

---

[4]Mitra, Nripendra Nath. 'The Indian Annual Register' July–December 1938, Vol. II, The Annual Register Office, p. 329, https://bit.ly/3hwLldW. Accessed on 28 February 2022.

[5]Bal, Hartosh Singh. 'The Takeover: How the RSS is Infiltrating India's Intellectual Spaces', *The Caravan*, 1 April 2019, https://bit.ly/3i0qqjv. Accessed on 11 March 2022.

philosophy behind the CAA and the Savarkar–Golwalkar school of thought would be disingenuous. In the end, it may lead to nothing: not a single Muslim may lose their citizenship as a result of the CAA and related proposals and, contrary to its critics, that may not even be its real purpose. But it has already had the effect of heightening the Muslim sense of insecurity about their future in India, which, in fact, may have been the real intention: to send a message to the community. An insecure minority, cowed into silence, is a perfect subject of the majoritarian rule.

Yet, in one sense, there was a twist to the script: it propelled a demoralized community into action in a manner that appeared to catch officials by surprise, particularly the way in which burkha-clad conservative women took to the streets using potent symbols of Indian nationalism to question the logic behind the CAA. The government gave the impression of scrambling to catch up, and rather than reach out to protesters, there was an attempt to demonize them as part of an anti-national 'Muslim insurgency' designed to benefit India's foreign enemies—an implicit reference to Pakistan. Senior BJP leaders lined up to denounce the movement with the then official spokesman and head of the BJP's IT cell calling it an 'Islamist insurgency' with foreign links.[6] He accused the protesters of getting their 'instructions

---

[6]@amitmalviya. Twitter, 1 April 2020, 1.48 a.m., https://bit.ly/35Ie8JF. Accessed on 28 February 2022.

from the masjid'.[7] He has also alleged that the agitation was being used as a pretext to radicalize Muslim youth, including little children.

Home Minister Amit Shah accused the protestors and their supporters of speaking the 'language of Imran Khan,'[8] and Prime Minister Narendra Modi said one could tell who the protesters were from 'the way they dress'.[9] It was also alleged that they were being bankrolled by shadowy outside sources. The BJP went on the offensive with its Muslim spokespersons—Mukhtar Abbas Naqvi, Shazia Ilmi and Shahnawaz Hussain alleging that the protesters were being manipulated by the 'enemies' of India.

Commentators saw it as part of a conscious strategy to fuel a culture war against Muslims. The problem with this strategy, noted an analyst, was that it risked further alienating a community which already felt under 'siege'.[10]

Encouraged by such rhetoric, some hotheads took to violence with two firing incidents reported within days

---

[7] Suroor, Hasan, 'BJfP's Rhetoric Against Shaheen Bagh May End Up Fuelling the Very Thing It Fears—Islamic Radicalism', *Scroll.in*, 7 February 2020, https://bit.ly/3tw4r9K. Accessed on 3 March 2022.

[8] Shali, Pooja, and Singh, Ram Kinkar. 'Arvind Kejriwal, Rahul Gandhi Speak Same Language As Imran Khan: Amit Shah', *India Today*, 24 January 2020, https://bit.ly/3C6Exgt. Accessed on 28 February 2022.

[9] Kiro, Santosh K. '"Look at Their Clothes": Modi Plays Communal Card on CAA, Targets Muslim Protestors', *The Wire,* 16 December 2019, https://bit.ly/3ptUdFx. Accessed on 28 February 2022.

[10] Suroor, Hasan, 'BJP's Rhetoric Against Shaheen Bagh May End Up Fuelling the Very Thing It Fears—Islamic Radicalism', *Scroll.in*, 7 February 2020, https://bit.ly/3tw4r9K. Accessed on 3 March 2022.

of each other in January–February 2020. In one, a man identified by police as Kapil Gujjar, allegedly shouted '*Jai Sri Ram*' as he fired shots standing near the protest site. NDTV reported that he was 'also heard saying: '*Humare desh mein sirf Hinduon ki chalegi aur kisi ki nahi* (In our country, only Hindus will prevail).'[11] Two days earlier, a teenaged boy fired a crude pistol at unarmed protesters with 'dozens of policemen behind him, watching'.[12] The incidents came barely days after a video showing the then Union Minister of State for Finance Anurag Thakur leading a crowd of BJP supporters into chants of '*Desh ke gaddaron ko, goli maro salon ko,* [Shoot the bloody traitors],' went viral.

The scenes were straight from the religious-centric nationalism playbook. According to historian S. Irfan Habib, to fully comprehend its current upsurge 'we need to go back to the three crucial decades of the 1920s, '30s and '40s of the freedom struggle.'[13] Its seeds, he writes, were actually sown 'in the midst of the excitement of the freedom struggle'. While the nationalism that emerged from the freedom struggle was inclusive, embracing India's religious, linguistic and cultural diversity, there were tendencies, both, among Hindus and Muslims—the so-called sectarian 'essentialists'—

---

[11]Shukla, Saurabh. 'Firing At Shaheen Bagh, Delhi's Second In 3 Days At An Anti-CAA Protest', NDTV, 1 February 2020, https://bit.ly/3HNw96S. Accessed on 2 March 2022.
[12]Ibid.
[13]Habib, S. Irfan. 'Introduction', S. Irfan Habib (ed.), *Indian Nationalism: The Essential Writings*, Aleph Book Company, 2017.

who wanted to polarize the country around religious and cultural identities, and impose their own monocultural idea of nationalism. The idea of a secular India, dubbed the 'Nehruvian Idea of India', was 'an anathema to those who conceived a nation around communitarian and regressive values—both Hindu and Muslim'.[14]

'The struggle between those trying to find unity in India's diversity and those seeking to compartmentalize India into different nations was intense from the early twentieth century onwards... It succeeded in dividing India', Prof. Habib writes, pointing out that the creation of Pakistan as a separate Muslim homeland generated an equally significant pressure to declare India a Hindu nation.[15]

The upshot is that there's nothing 'sudden' about the resurgence of Hindu nationalism. It's a hangover of the competitive faith-centric Hindu–Muslim nationalism of pre-Independence India. A fact that has always rankled with Hindu nationalists is that while Muslim religious nationalists succeeded in achieving their aim of carving out a separate Muslim nation, they failed in their push for a 'Hindu India'. A secular India, in which the Muslim minority enjoys the same rights as the Hindu majority has, therefore, been a running sore for Hindu nationalists. The CAA is a manifestation of Savarkar's Hindutva principle of Hindu supremacy.

---
[14]Ibid.
[15]Ibid.

According to academic and political analyst, Shiv Visvanathan, 'Majoritarianism in India has combined with a jingoist nationalism... The transition from nationalism of the independence movement, which was a costume ball of ideas, to the uniformity of the nation state is complete.'[16]

Historically, there have been two broad strands of Indian nationalism—the inclusive mainstream nationalism of the INC, and faith-based Hindu and Muslim nationalisms championed by the Hindu Mahasabha-RSS, and the Muslim League, respectively. So, the battle lines between 'secular' and 'communal' forces were drawn long before Independence, indeed, quite early during the freedom struggle. Hindu and Muslim nationalisms fed on each other in their common opposition to the Congress party, which also faced resistance from Hindu revivalists, such as Lala Lajpat Rai, Bal Gangadhar Tilak and Bipin Chandra Pal, all of whom, as Prof. Habib notes, were 'deeply engaged in imagining an Indian nation and nationalism with Hinduism as the fulcrum...'[17] Leaders like Sardar Patel and Govind Ballabh Pant, among others, also did not share Nehru's enthusiasm for western style secularism. Historians have written of 'resistance' by the wider society to the Congress brand of liberal, big-tent nationalism suggesting that Hindu

---

[16]Visvanathan, Shiv. 'The Paranoid Art of Nationalism', *The Hindu*, 26 August 2016, https://bit.ly/3hrwul3. Accessed on 28 February 2022.
[17]Habib, S. Irfan. 'Introduction', S. Irfan Habib (ed.), *Indian Nationalism: The Essential Writings*, Aleph Book Company, 2017.

and Muslim nationalists were more in tune with the mood of their respective constituencies. Significant sections of both Hindu and Muslim communities were said to prefer communitarian nationalism centred on communities rather than one-size-fits all secularism.

Despite their mutual public hostility, Right-wing Hindu and Muslim nationalists represented two sides of the same communal coin; so much so, that the Hindu Mahasabha and Muslim League ran joint coalition governments in several provinces, notably Sindh, the erstwhile North-West Frontier Province (NWFP) and Bengal, in the late 1930s and early 1940s, after the Congress ministries resigned in response to Mahatma Gandhi's call to broaden and intensify non-cooperation with the colonial government ahead of the 1942 Quit India Movement. In 1937, Hindu Mahasabha members joined Ghulam Hussain Hidayatullah's Muslim League government in Sindh. Four years later, the Sindh Government became the first Provincial Assembly to pass an official resolution endorsing the League's claim that 'Muslims of India are a separate nation', and backing the creation of Pakistan. Despite its public opposition to partition, the Hindu Mahasabha ministers remained in the government 'content' with a token protest when the resolution was passed.[18]

In 1941, Dr Shyama Prasad Mookerjee, the second in command of the Hindu Mahasabha joined A.K. Fazlul Huq's

---

[18]Noorani, Abdul Gafoor Abdul Majeed. *The RSS and the BJP: A Division of Labour*, LeftWord Books, 2000.

Muslim League ministry in Bengal as finance minister and remained in the ministry after it moved the Lahore Resolution. Only a year before, Huq had moved the 'Pakistan Resolution' which committed the Muslim League to a separate Muslim nation prompting the Congress party to call him a communalist. In 1943, the Hindu Mahasabha partnered with the Muslim League to form a government in the NWFP.

These are hard verifiable and well-documented facts of history. The narrative that Hindu and Muslim nationalists were sworn enemies is a myth. They are often referred to as 'strange bedfellows' thrown together by political opportunism. But, in reality, there was nothing 'strange' about it: the alacrity with which Hindu and Muslim nationalists jumped into bed only shows that they had more in common than what divided them. Most importantly, they shared an ideological affinity. Both supported the two-nation theory; both opposed the call for the Quit India Movement; and both frequently collaborated with the colonial administration. Central to the Mahasabha–League philosophy was the notion of 'one religion, one culture, one language'. They regarded this as the basis of nationhood.

> The Hindu Mahasabha wanted a country for Hindus speaking Hindi while the Muslim League preferred to have a country of Urdu-speaking Muslims. By doing so, both organisations also adopted the principle of

having a 'common enemy'. For instance, the Hindu Mahasabha considered Pakistan (read Muslims) as its common enemy while the Muslim League hated India (read Hindus), mistaking a secular nation as the homeland of Hindus.[19]

For all its official opposition to the division of India, the Hindu Mahasabha helped the argument for Partition by making political alliances with Muslim League. I have said it before, but it bears reiteration that far from being enemies, they were ideological twins, joined at the hip in their single-minded pursuit of their respective goals, even if it meant collaborating with colonial rulers. Both threw their weight behind the British crackdown on the Congress party and benefited from it. The Hindu Mahasabha took an official stance when, in his presidential address at the Kanpur session of the Mahasabha in 1942, Savarkar defended the decision calling it a policy of 'responsive co-operation' even as he denounced the Congress as a 'pseudo-nationalist body'. Historian Shamsul Islam has chronicled at length the Hindu Mahasabha's flirtation with colonial rulers in *Hindu Nationalism and Rashtriya Swayamsevak Sangh*. According to academic Jyotirmaya Sharma, Savarkar's 'commitment to the creation of a Hindu Rashtra superseded the goal of

---

[19]Laliwala, Sharik. 'During the Quit India Movement, the Hindu Mahasabha Played the British Game', *The Wire*, 8 August 2019, https://bit.ly/3tokh5Y. Accessed on 28 February 2022.

political independence of India.'[20]

That Savarkar's ideological successors should now appropriate the mantle of 'nationalism' has more than a touch of irony. It is rewriting history. As Laliwala pointed out, 'At this crucial juncture in India's polity, it is important to know this dishonourable genealogy of the Hindutva ideologues with which the present-day Hindu Right-wing is associated.'[21]

Rise of Muslim Nationalism

Muslim nationalists and their main vehicle, the Muslim League, benefited both from the actions of the Hindu Mahasabha and the Congress party. We saw before how the Hindu Mahasabha, driven by its opposition to the Congress party, made common cause with the League, contributing to their separatist agenda. The Congress party, on the other hand, helped them ironically by its intransigent approach to them, especially its repudiation of the 1916 Lucknow Pact with the Muslim League on giving Muslims more say in governance. The role of the Congress party's leadership in strengthening Jinnah's hands to push ahead with his Pakistan agenda is well-documented.

---

[20]Sharma, Jyotirmaya. *Hindutva: Exploring the Idea of Hindu Nationalism*, HarperCollins, 2015.
[21]Laliwala, Sharik. 'During the Quit India Movement, the Hindu Mahasabha Played the British Game', *The Wire*, 8 August 2019, https://bit.ly/3tokh5Y. Accessed on 28 February 2022.

Many in India—and all our textbooks—hold Jinnah solely responsible for the split. It is time we acknowledged what the best of our historians already know, that he was not the only one to blame for that wretched event. Others—the British, the Congress, the Hindu Mahasabha—were equally, if not more, complicit.[22]

The Congress party's attitude towards the League hardened, especially after its sweeping victory in the 1937 provincial elections. One of the major reasons for this was the lack of personal rapport between top Congress leaders, particularly, Nehru and Jinnah. Despite their shared cosmopolitan outlook there was an intense mutual dislike between them. This went back to when Jinnah was a Congressman and Nehru saw him as a rival for the top job after Independence. The Dalai Lama has claimed that Gandhi was willing to give the prime ministership to Jinnah, and that this would have averted Partition. 'I think it was a little bit self-centred attitude of Pandit Nehru that he should be the prime minister... Mahatma Gandhi's thinking, if it had materialised, then India, Pakistan would have been united', the Dalai Lama said addressing an event at the Goa Institute of Management.[23]

---

[22]Balakrishnan, Uday. 'Who's Responsible for India's Partition?', *Business Line*, 31 May 2018, https://bit.ly/3hxwoZc. Accessed on 28 February 2022.
[23]Malkarnekar, Gauree. 'India & Pak Would Have Stayed United But for Nehru: Dalai Lama', *The Times of India*, 9 August 2018, https://bit.ly/3MuJpRu. Accessed on 2 March 2022.

While there is no historical evidence to back Dalai Lama's claim, at the same time there is no denying that the Congress was most reluctant to make any concessions to Jinnah. British military historian, Barney White-Spunner has written: 'Had Congress reacted more favourably to Jinnah's approaches in 1937, then things might have turned out differently'.[24]

The Congress was most reluctant to make any concessions to Jinnah. After the 1937 elections, the party had started to believe that, in fact, it had no reason to do so, given that the League had been routed. While the Congress party won in eight of the 11 provinces where elections were held, the League drew a blank. The Muslims' concern was their gross under-representation in public services, which had been a long-standing demand, much before Jinnah came into the picture and weaponized it for the League's political aims. Ordinary Muslims, most of whom voted for the Congress party, had great expectations from the party, and were, therefore, deeply disappointed when it failed to address their concerns. To build his case for a separate Muslim homeland, Jinnah was able to tap into Muslim anger and fuel the community's fears that Muslims would not get a fair deal in India after the British left. The issue of representation, as Uday Balakrishnan points out, lay at the heart of Jinnah's campaign that eventually led to the partition. It had 'a long history going back to 1906 when a demand for it was first

---

[24]White-Spunner, Barney. *Partition: The Story of Indian Independence And The Creation of Pakistan in 1947*, Simon & Schuster UK, 2017.

made on behalf of Muslims by a delegation led by the Agha Khan to the Viceroy'.[25]

> Jinnah bought into it much later and even arrived at a pact with the Congress. Few today know that the Lucknow Pact, as it was popularly known, was arrived at in a joint session of the Congress and the Muslim League in 1916. Jinnah who played a major role in getting the pact through, was hailed as an apostle of Hindu-Muslim unity by Sarojini Naidu. It was the Congress that later repudiated the pact.[26]

Jinnah never forgave the Congress party for what he saw as a 'betrayal', a view that found echo even among moderate Muslims. The Congress party's attitude after the 1937 elections deepened the trust deficit and further alienated the Muslim community, giving an unstoppable momentum to their demand for a new homeland. There's a view that Nehru's antipathy towards Jinnah and refusal to compromise was as much, if not more, responsible for Partition as Jinnah's actions.

The rest is history. American writer Nisid Hajari, author of *Midnight's Furies: The Deadly Legacy of India's Partition*, asked by an Indian interviewer who he thought was to blame for the events that led to partition, said:

---

[25]Balakrishnan, Uday. 'Who's Responsible for India's Partition?', *Business Line*, 31 May 2018, https://bit.ly/3hxwoZc. Accessed on 28 February 2022.
[26]Ibid.

> Personality-wise, Nehru was more charming than Jinnah; even Jinnah's friends would admit that. But in terms of who is responsible for the mistakes—and ruining the chance of political compromise—I think, in that case Nehru was at least as much to blame as Jinnah.
>
> Jinnah was arguing the case like the lawyer he was. Nehru had multiple chances to make compromises, that would have preserved a united India, and he chose not to... I think Jinnah had very good reasons not to trust Nehru and the Congress and that is Nehru's fault.[27]

Noted Pakistani historian Ayesha Jalal has been consistently vocal on this issue and has incurred the wrath of even many liberal Indians, who have called her a Jinnah apologist. I have dwelt at some length on the Nehru–Jinnah factor only to underline how Right-wing Muslim nationalists ended up winning the day against their own expectations, thanks to a little help from the Congress party on the one hand, and the Hindu Mahasabha on the other. Jinnah, did not as much win, as he was handed victory on a platter by secular nationalists and the Hindu Right through purely selfish reasons. The Congress party did it to get rid of a difficult political rival (Jinnah), and the Hindu Mahasabha to undermine the Congress party, and show its loyalty to its British patrons. The British, of course, were the ones pulling

---

[27] Daniel, Vaihayasi Pande. "'Nehru Was As Much to Blame As Jinnah for Partition.'" *reddif.com*, 29 January 2008, https://bit.ly/35TzUKy. Accessed on 2 March 2022.

the strings and running the show. They wanted a Muslim Pakistan as a counterbalance to a Hindu India so they could leverage both after they left. And they did.

'Good' Nationalism and 'Bad' Nationalism

It will be no exaggeration to argue that the state of Hindu–Muslim relations since Independence is a legacy of the self-serving nationalistic politics played out during the freedom struggle. It generated so much toxicity that Gandhi was prompted to ask: 'Is hatred essential for nationalism?' The answer he must have wanted to hear was a reassuring 'No'. But, alas, history has answered it differently. Nationalism and religion—mostly overlapping—have been the biggest source of hatred between the two communities. The two World Wars, the Holocaust, the Irish Civil War (1922–23); The Troubles (1968–98), the 30-year-long bloody conflict between Catholic Irish nationalists and Protestant British nationalists (aka Unionists); the running sore of Jewish–Palestinian conflict; India's partition; the 1971 break-up of Pakistan which led to the formation of Bangladesh; the Bosnian Genocide (1992–95), are only some of the more recent examples of the hatred provoked in the name of faith-induced nationalism.

Rabindranath Tagore described nationalism as 'a great menace'. He wrote that though he had grown up being taught that 'idolatry of the Nation is almost better than reverence for God... I've outgrown that teaching, and it is my conviction that my countrymen will truly gain their India by fighting against the education which teaches them that a country is greater than the ideals of humanity'.[28]

Sardar Vallabhbhai Patel warned against the danger that nationalism posed to a newly independent India. In a speech in Madras in 1949 that would resonate with many in India today, he said:

> We in the Government have been dealing with the RSS movement. They want that Hindu Rajya or Hindu culture should be imposed by force. No government can tolerate this. There are almost as many Muslims in this country as in the part that has been partitioned away. We are not going to drive them away. It would be an evil day we started that game...[29]

Dr B.R. Ambedkar was so concerned about the emerging contours of nationalism that, 'in the context of the nationalism debate today, Ambedkar would have been an anti-national', Prof Habib notes in his volume of writings on Indian nationalism, which includes a short piece published by Dr Ambedkar after he founded the Independent Labour Party in 1936. He wrote: 'If nationalism means the worship of the ancient past—the discarding of everything that is

---

[28]Tagore, Rabindranath. *Nationalism*, Macmillan and Co. Limited, London, 1918, p. 107.
[29]Habib, S. Irfan. 'Introduction', *Indian Nationalism: The Essential Writings*, Aleph Book Company, 2017.

not local in origin and colour—then Labour cannot accept nationalism as its creed.'[30]

Likewise, Maulana Abul Kalam countered separatist Muslim nationalism declaring his belief in what he called 'indivisible nationalism'. Political scientists and historians hesitate to lump all nationalists in the 'rotten eggs' basket, and tend to draw a distinction between 'good' nationalists, such as Tagore, Nehru Patel, Azad, and 'bad' nationalists such as Savarkar, Golwalkar, Jinnah, etc., arguing that nationalism per se is not a bad thing; it can even be a noble sentiment, as was witnessed during the Indian freedom struggle, when all Indians, irrespective of religion, caste or creed united under the banner of Indian nationalism to fight colonial rule. But in reality, examples of 'good' nationalism are few and far between. Historically, 'bad' nationalism has held sway, and is increasingly becoming the norm from the US and Eastern Europe to Britain, China and South Asia—including, of course, India. There are valid fears that much of the world is hurtling towards some variant of 'bad' nationalism.

Albert Einstein called nationalism 'an infantile disease' and 'the measles of mankind'.[31] Nearly a century later, that definition still holds good.

---

[30]Ibid.
[31]Viereck, George Sylvester. 'What Life Means to Einstein: An Interview with George Sylvester Viereck', *The Saturday Evening Post*, 26 October 1929, https://bit.ly/3IPTpST. Accessed on 2 March 2022.

6

Ordinary Indians Speak Out

In the following pages, ordinary concerned citizens of India cutting across faiths and political affiliations candidly express their views on how they see the current crisis in secularism, its impact on Hindu–Muslim relations and the way forward.

Failed by Secularism, but Not Defeated

Moinuddin Ahmad

The electoral success of AIMIM in the 2020 Bihar Assembly elections—its first significant successful electoral foray outside its stronghold in Hyderabad—has sent alarm bells ringing in secularist quarters, with its growing popularity seen as a threat to secularism, and conversely, a boost to communal politics. Its leader, Asaduddin Owaisi, has been compared to Jinnah, often unfairly portrayed as having been solely responsible for India's partition. AIMIM has clearly sent a message that it means business. Even the Kerala-based Indian Union Muslim League (IUML) was not able to create the kind of ripple effect that AIMIM has been able to, in recent years.

Its adversaries accuse it of engaging in communal politics, luring Muslim voters away from the secular parties, and thus, strengthening majoritarian voices in India. While concern over the threat posed to secularism by sectarian forces like AIMIM is understandable, the question to be asked is: why does a small regional party with a paltry presence in national politics seem to be doing so well? If its rise is really a sign that secularism is on the wane in India, then the next question must be, 'Why is it so? Did something go wrong? If yes, were there any flaws in the way it was practiced? And, is it fair to blame Muslim political parties for the crisis of secularism in India?'

Indian secularism is ridden with complications and contradictions at the conceptual level. Separating the state from faiths might have looked desirable, but it was arguably not a practical choice for a deeply religious country. Historian Partha Chatterjee, in his essay, 'Secularism and Toleration', noted two contradictions in India's secular politics. According to him, even while professing to be a secular state it ended up—for various historical reasons—regulating, funding and even administering various religious institutions. Second, while minority communities were allowed to keep their personal laws and rights to run their institutions, there was no clarity on how it would work in a secular state where, theoretically, a common secular law was supposed to govern all communities.

In the absence of a France-like concept of *laïcité* and a constant connection with the religious institutions, it was impossible for the Indian state to remain secular in classical terms. In the event, Indian secularism was reduced to being akin to an equal opportunities employer—more understood in terms of extending equal treatment to all the faiths, and, in the end, Hindus as the largest faith group effectively became the first among equals. Secularism in India did not have strong foundations since its very conception, with concessions given to various communities at various points in time. It has always lived on the edge with politicians flirting with different religious groups for electoral gains, and in the process eroding the core ideas of secularism. Any pretence was finally given up after the victory of the BJP in the 2014 general elections. Backed by the RSS, an avowed advocate of Hindu Rashtra, the government led by Narendra Modi ushered in a new phase of muscular majoritarianism—the idea that Hindus alone are 'real' Indians, signalling further marginalization of religious minorities.

In Search of Equality

At the time of Partition, a large number of Muslims chose to stay in India because they trusted the erstwhile leadership that promised equal rights to all the citizens, in what would become a democratic state with an overwhelming Hindu majority. Despite the communally charged situation, they rejected the invitations and appeals of fellow Muslims who were leaving for Pakistan. Fortune, however, doesn't seem to have favoured the brave, in this particular case.

Seven decades later, millions of Muslims are at the risk of losing their citizenship if they fail to prove their nationality in front of a tribunal. They have been dubbed 'illegal immigrants', and there are plans to strip them of their citizenship by using the CAA and the NRC. When Muslims protested, they faced brutal police crackdown. In Northeast Delhi, their demand for constitutional rights was branded communal. Actual communal riots followed, in which Muslims suffered major losses.

All that Muslims are seeking is to be treated as equal citizens and with respect. There is a deep sense of disillusionment, especially among Muslim millennials, and they are ready to challenge any policy that seeks to exclude them or degrades them vis-à-vis their compatriots from the majority community.

The winter of 2019 will be remembered for the countrywide anti-CAA protests spearheaded by young

Muslims who believe in the Indian constitution, even as they are proud of their religious faith. A new kind of Muslim leadership is evolving—one that is unapologetic about faith and bold in negotiating the terms of engagement with other political parties. They call out the so-called secular parties that have used Muslim votes for political gains as they continue to question and repel forces of majoritarianism. We are witnessing the birth of a 'new' Muslim who is ready to assert their constitutional rights and challenge attempts to deny them their rightful place in their own country.

Moinuddin Ahmad is a journalist and researcher.

Notions of Secularism

Irfanullah Farooqi

A series of reflections by public intellectuals in the past few years suggest that Indian secularism is dying a slow death, or, at least, it has ceased to exist in its spirit in state–society transactions, election campaigns, inter-community relations, public policies, and, perhaps what is more worrying, legislation judicial interventions and verdicts. This gradual de-secularization of everyday life, we are informed, has raised questions about India's claim as a democratic nation committed to equality and social justice for all of its citizens. This concern is not to be taken lightly. Something exceedingly prized is at stake here: our capacity as human beings to understand the other, care for them and strive for their overall well-being.

Secularism emerged in Europe because of the way the unholy alliance between the church and the state was suffocating public life. It was a response to excesses committed, not merely in the name of religion, but *of* religion itself. India's experience with religion, however, has been very different. We have not had a single ruler imposing a state religion. Our history, as opposed to Europe's, does not make us sceptical about religion's role in public life. Indian secularism—committed to freedom, equality and protection of every citizen's fundamental rights—emerged amidst deep religious diversity against the backdrop of horrific Partition violence. Although the word 'secular' was added to the Preamble of the Constitution only in 1976, India's allegiance to secularism goes back much further. Even during the colonial rule, a blueprint of Indian secularism was taking shape. Late 1930s onwards, the mainstream nationalist politics represented by the Congress party, responding to untouchability, women's rights and worrying state of Hindu–Muslim relations, took an inherently secular position. By declaring their principled opposition to both intra and inter-religious domination, leaders like Jawaharlal Nehru sought to pitch a secular politics that aspired for social freedom.

Notwithstanding its inspiring history and indubitable uniqueness, why has Indian secularism not succeeded in bringing various communities together, more specifically Hindus and Muslims? For all the talk about our composite culture—the so-called Ganga–Jamni tehzeeb and shared histories, etc.—the fact is that the two communities remain apart, and that is a clear failure of Indian secularism. A number of reasons are offered for this, but what stands out is the state's sheer disinterestedness in promoting secularism. Many Indians are not even aware what secularism really means with the word 'secular' mostly seen as being anti-religion, and opposed to traditions and social customs. Think of remarks such as *'Zyada secularpana na jhaado* [Don't throw around this secular attitude]', *'Dher secular na bano*

[Don't play secular with me]', or *Zyada secular ho gaye ho* [You have become too secular]', in response to anything that suggests an open-mindedness resulting in 'deviance'. Very often, someone who stops following religious obligations or becomes somewhat irregular in that respect is immediately called secular, rather than agnostic. Needless to say, in a country like India, where almost every domain of human activity is touched by religion, a misconception of this kind is bound to have serious repercussions.

For quite some time now, Indian secularism has been primarily looked at from the vantage point of state–society relations. In that respect, we have been more focused on the ins and outs of a secular state. However, given the rise of communal hatred and violence in recent years, it is, perhaps, desirable that we look at secularism in terms of inter-community relations. In doing so, we will be able to shift our focus from secular state to something that is much more promising—secular society.

Focusing on Indian secularism solely from the vantage point of inter-community relations, how do we make sense of relations between Hindus and Muslims, something that has got much worse in recent years? Hindus constitute around 79 per cent of India's population whereas Muslims are approximately 15 per cent. Given how phenomenally one outnumbers the other, ideally speaking, there should not have been any rivalry between the two. However, there remain strands of history and expressions of culture that are invoked every now and then to pitch one in hostile opposition to the other. Attempts by Right-wing Hindu nationalists to portray one as the political, cultural and historical 'other' have had astounding electoral success.

So how do we make sense of this growing antagonism between the two communities, this growing feeling that the interests of one are in absolute opposition to the other? More than anything else, it is to do with absence of trust and faith in each other. Each is fearful of the other. However, are we to treat the fear of both the communities alike? The fear of 15 per cent of a society cannot be treated at par with the fear of the dominant 79 per cent. It is, however, common and must be our starting point if a principled secular living is to be attained. For example, the fear among Hindus that Muslims will wipe out their community is plainly unfounded. But, in the current political climate, it is harder to dismiss Muslim fears about a surge in populist Right-wing Hindu politics based on hostility towards minority rights.

The truth is that the future of Indian secularism is in the hands of the Hindus, for the simple reason that they form the majority and hold the levers of power—just as in a Muslim-majority country, the buck stops with Muslims. Only Hindus can save the idea of a pluralistic and tolerant India from becoming a casualty of a narrow sectarian politics. If Hindus could do their part we could achieve what Dr B.R. Ambedkar called 'an associated mode of living'. The alternative—the unchecked rise of majoritarianism—leaves

Muslims with no other option but to simply accept their status as second-class citizens in the interest of their safety and protection. Meanwhile, the growing political alienation among Muslims is an issue that lies outside the ambit of secularism. Muslims are demanding that they should be recognized *as* Muslims. It is a call for a very different kind of knowing and understanding, one that is strikingly transformative. In embarking on this transformative understanding, Hindus can educate the rest of the world in what secularism and democracy can offer to the modern world.

To be sure, the progress report of Indian secularism is not satisfactory. We stand at the cusp of one of the most defining moments of our nationhood, and where we go from here depends on whether we are willing to rise above manufactured animosities and invest in an ethically informed understanding of the other, or embrace sectarian populism. But, then, the choice need not necessarily be binary and should not keep us away from what Jacques Derrida beautifully phrased in his book *The Politics of Friendship* as the 'radical experience of the perhaps'. Perhaps, it will all end well, finally.

Irfanullah Farooqi is an assistant professor at South Asian University.

Secular India—Lost in Transition

Uzma Azhar Ali

Secularism is not the same thing as 'secularization'. The former involves separation of religion from the state while the latter seeks to push religion out of public sphere altogether—a socio-cultural process that has taken different forms in different countries. Historically, most Western European governments opted for 'secularization', while India went in for a secular order where the state was meant to maintain a neutral distance from different religions in a multi-religious society.

It was only in 1976 that 'secularism' was inserted in the Preamble of the Constitution, but the Indian state practised a form of secularism since Independence, and sought to acknowledge, encourage and promote cultural diversity 'through cultural rights of minorities; the funding of minority educational institutions; the cultural rights of indigenous peoples; linguistic rights; the self-government rights of culturally distinct groups; asymmetrical federalism; legal pluralism; affirmative action for marginalized groups etc.'[1] Before that, secularism had virtually no roots in the Indian society and even less so in Indian polity. Gandhi espoused a

---

[1] Bhargava, Rajeev. 'India's Model: Faith, Secularism and Democracy,' *openDemocracy*, 3 November 2004, https://bit.ly/3pwfqP0. Accessed on 28 January 2022.

syncretic, tolerant pluralism in the context of Indian society carrying forward the legacy of the Mughal Empire.

But here is the thing: even as the Congress party opted for secularism, many of its leaders—from pre-Partition days to the Babri Masjid demolition—have practised a form of 'soft' communal politics as opposed to the BJP's hard Hindutva line of politics. The BJP's rise to power shows how significant the role of religion is in electoral politics in India. The Ayodhya Ram Mandir campaign continues to pay dividends for the BJP while the Congress party tries to have its foot in both the camps—keeping up the appearance of a liberal 'secular' party while also quietly playing the soft Hindu card. Emotional appeal of religion has seen Modi win with two-thirds majority in the Lok Sabha and it may be difficult to defeat him given the prevailing climate of majoritarianism. It has exposed the shallow roots of Indian secularism with key institutions—legislature, executive, police, the media and sections of the judiciary—having been compromised.

During communal riots over the years (1984, 1992–93, 2002), we have seen the police stand with the majority community and often even give rioters a free hand (Hashimpura [1987], Bhagalpur [1989], Muzaffarnagar [2013], Northeast Delhi riots [2020], etc.) Ordinary policeman acting as a person of faith rather than a neutral enforcer of law in the times of conflict reveals the nature of vulnerability and weakness of Indian secularism.

Violence against minorities has palpably increased, with the perpetrators being allowed to get away with impunity. The media, which should have raised issues and highlighted the excesses being done in the name of religion, has instead, helped fan the flames of hate and division. When the police attacked students of JMI and AMU protesting against discriminatory CAA on 15 December 2019, most media channels chose to echo police claims, accusing students of rowdyism and destroying public property. Muslim students were also blamed for the riots in Northeast Delhi in January 2020 whereas the real culprits who made hate speeches and incited violence, still roam free.

In March 2020, Tablighi Jamaat was blamed by the media for spreading 'corona jihad' without an iota of proof.[2] The abrogation of Article 370, which protected the special status of the Muslim-majority Kashmir Valley, and the harassment of young Muslim men under the new 'love jihad' laws enacted by several BJP-ruled states are just additional tools in the already impressive arsenal of the Hindu right to further the persecution of young Muslim men. Questioning the nationalist credentials of not just ordinary Muslims, but of celebrities such as Bollywood actor, Aamir Khan, shows how fast the virus of majoritarian nationalism is spreading. The fact is that India never practised a strict separation of

---

[2]Sharma, Ayan and Gupta, Chahak. 'Audit of Bigotry: How Indian Media Vilified Tablighi Jamaat Over Coronavirus Outbreak', *Newslaundry*, 27 April 2020, https://bit.ly/3sKTyl0. Accessed on 3 February 2022.

state and religion, but of late, the lines have blurred even more. To be sure, religion and culture are deeply embedded in the Indian psyche and society. But India also has a long tradition of religious and cultural pluralism that has enriched Indian society. It is the co-existence of diverse religions that gives Indian society its unique character. In the words of Urdu poet Majrooh Sultanpuri:

Mujh se kahā jibrīl-e-junūñ ne ye bhī vahi-e-ilāhī hai
Mazhab to bas mazhab-e-dil hai baaqī sab gumrāhī hai

[As Gabriel said, religion is the only religion of the heart; rest is deflection].

Dr Uzma Azhar Ali is a researcher and teacher.

Secularism and Nationalism

Zarine Khan

In India, secularism has become a euphemism for minority appeasement by the state in a pejorative sense. The opposite of secularism is deemed to be nationalism: two fundamentally western concepts that have put the idea of India under immense pressure. While secularism was intended to preserve India's diversity, nationalism has become a short-hand for demanding conformity, with no room for divergence. Managing to displace 'communal' as the opposing binary of 'secular' is quite a feat for the Hindu Right. Once upon a time, both Hindus and Muslims faced accusations of being communal, but now, miraculously Hindus have absolved themselves of any role in communalizing Hindu–Muslim relations portraying only Muslims as communal—a community which thinks only about its own interests and is ready to kill for it. Hindus, on the other hand, represent the nation and are truly nationalist.

Hindu–Muslim relations in India are increasingly being shaped by the alleged culpability of Muslims. The mainstream discourse driven by the capitalist-nationalist media and amplified by social media is obsessed with the idea of the 'un-Indian' (read 'anti-national') Muslim—the jihadist, the criminal, the rapist, the wife-beater, the deceptive lover seducing Hindu girls for the purpose of converting them to

Islam. Every conceivable ethical and moral wrongdoing is sought to be linked to Islam and its followers. One rotten act by an individual Muslim is amplified into 'national rage'. Islamophobia is rampant and enjoys a not-so-covert state legitimacy through hastily legislated laws dressed up in nationalistic rhetoric that actually target Muslims alone. Whether it is an obviously systematic assault on Muslims or a riot, any state investigation invariably ends up blaming Muslims.

This brings us to the question: what is the place of Muslims in India? And why is the Hindu Right so keen to 'put them in their place'? The first question relates to the nature of the Indian state (secular) and the second question to that of the Indian society (religious). The Indian state was meant to *be* secular and Indians were expected to *become* secular. On 24 January 1948, Prime Minister Jawaharlal Nehru visited AMU amidst calls for its shutdown as it was the epicentre of Muslim separatism. An atmosphere of fear prevailed. His visit was meant to assure Muslims who stayed back in India that the Indian state was committed to treat all its citizens equally, and it was for them to commit themselves towards a secular state. Disregarding the students' previous allegiances, he told them, 'Do not think that you are outsiders here, for you are as much flesh and blood of India as anyone else, and you have every right to share in what India has to offer'.³ The limits of this secularization, however, soon became apparent with the reconstruction of Somnath Temple with the blessings of the office bearers of the Indian state. Nehru's unease regarding President Dr Rajendra Prasad inaugurating the temple reflected the spirit of the Indian constitution. Nevertheless, Dr Prasad chose to go ahead with the inauguration, and this act reflected the inadequacy of Indian secularism.

Meanwhile, the BJP narrative about Muslims is rooted in a sense of resentment that is more perceived than real. Yet, the 'majority under attack' discourse has proved persuasive enough as the glue that binds its voters together. So, accusing a party like the AIMIM of hurting secular interests is disingenuous, especially as it claims to be committed to the Indian constitution and secularism. Some liberals in a hurry to appear objective, equate the politics of the BJP with that of the AIMIM. To present the AIMIM as anti-secular implies that no Muslim-led party is capable of working in everyone's interests while a Hindu nationalist party like the BJP or its parent organization, the RSS, is. The not-so-subtle messaging is that Muslims are incapable of being secular. This is an extension of the argument that Hindu fundamentalism is a reaction to Muslim fundamentalism, thus holding Muslims responsible for the current state of Hindu–Muslim relations.

The only way out of this impasse seems to be to

---

³'Freeing the Spirit of Man: Nehru on Communalism, Theocracy and Pakistan', *The Hindu*, 30 December 2019, https://bit.ly/3ty1pl5. Accessed on 3 March 2022.

deconstruct the image of religious Muslims as regressive and communal. If a devout, yet secular Hindu is able to appreciate the fact that a devout Muslim too can be secular, it will go a long way in building a society that celebrates both its religiosity and secular temper. A religious yet secular India need not be a contradiction, but a symbol of a diverse India where a secular Hindu and a secular Muslim, who are both devout believers of their respective religions, can co-exist peacefully with the help of a constitution that enables them to do so.

Zarine Khan is a research scholar.

India Needs 'Spiritual' Secularism

Avijit Pathak

In a country like ours, characterized by mind-boggling diversities and differences, the state can retain its legitimacy only if it does not favour or discriminate against people on the basis of caste, language, ethnicity, religion or any other cultural marker. Second, it is absolutely important to overcome the walls of separation caused by the ghettoization of the mind and space because cross-cultural or cross-religious interaction is possible only in a shared or inclusive realm of communication. And third, irrespective of cultural or religious differences, we all need to cherish and sustain a set of shared principles—human dignity, gender sensitivity and politico-intellectual freedom—for creating a world based on empathy, compassion and the art of listening. Yes, it is in this sense that I am an adherent champion of secularism.

But I have a problem with secularism if it is equated with what is known in the social sciences as 'non-reflexive modernity', an obsessive stress on scientific explanation and rationalization, and a corresponding decline in emphasis on religious worldview. It tends to create all sorts of hierarchical dualities: science vs spirituality, politics vs ethics and phenomenal vs transcendental. It has to be realized that if secularism is not nurtured by deep religiosity or spirituality, it might degenerate into a mere hedonistic doctrine of techno-economic progress pursued by ethically impoverished atomized individuals. Furthermore, an abstracted discourse of 'reason' or intellectualized idioms like 'liberty', 'equality' and 'fraternity' alone cannot sustain the foundations of human solidarity. (Possibly, Dr B.R. Ambedkar's turn towards Gautam Buddha revealed this truth.) Our secularism is likely to be shallow if it remains limited merely to a legal or constitutional provision. We need the healing power of religiosity to transform our inner world and move towards a world filled with the spirit of egalitarian cultural pluralism, or fundamental oneness amid apparent differences relating to rituals or theological doctrines. In other words, I am pleading for spiritually regenerated secularism—something beyond the politics of exclusivist organized religions or the scientism of soulless modernity.

What Is Spiritual Secularism?

Let me explain what I mean by religiosity or spiritual quest. I do not equate it with organized religions; nor do I equate it with the heavy baggage of ritualism or external symbols that the orthodox priest craft or clergy wants to sustain. I do admit that many of us see ourselves as 'Hindus', 'Muslims', 'Sikhs' or 'Christians', and we follow a set of rituals or practices to reaffirm our religious identities. And generally, we are conditioned; we just follow a brigade of 'followers'. Quite often, these organized religions create boundaries and walls of separation. Furthermore, many of these organized religions are not free from orthodoxy, caste and patriarchal violence.

So, religiosity or spiritual quest must be distinguished from the experience of being just a 'Hindu' or a 'Muslim'. It's a quest for the union of the phenomenal and the transcendental, finite and infinite. It is about love and compassion. It doesn't seek to impose one-size-fits-all uniformity, but breaks the walls of separation, and creates the possibility of non-discrimination, equity and solidarity. No fundamentalist doctrine can capture it. Fundamentalism is based on fear; it is non-dialogic and inherently violent. And hence, the religiosity I am propagating is against all sorts of communalism (an ugly politics based on one's ascriptive religious identity) or ghettoization. It would not be difficult for a spiritual person to walk with Tagore and Rumi, Jesus and Buddha, and Kabir and Nizamuddin Auliya. Hence, it would abhor the idea of a Hindu state or Muslim state or Christian state—or militant nationalism.

It's important to contextualize the entire debate. Yes, we carry the trauma of Partition: the psychic, moral and cultural wound it caused, or the way it brutalized our consciousness. We also carry the burden of divisive ideologies—from Savarkar's Hindutva to Jinnah's Muslim nationalism. And, not to forget the current politics of assertive Hindutva or majoritarian nationalism and the resultant Islamophobia. Under these circumstances, the debate on secularism has acquired a new meaning. Well, the dominant discourse of Hindu nationalism loathes the 'liberal/left' or 'Nehurivian/Marxist' notion of secularism. It is seen as 'elitist', 'anti-Hindu' and 'western'. But then, it is no less hostile to Gandhi's religiosity, spiritualized politics, cross-cultural dialogue and fusion of horizons. As nationalism is equated with Hindutva, it constructs its 'enemies'—Muslims as potential traitors, or 'urban Naxals' as 'pseudo-secular' leftists.

How do we combat it? The problem is that what these days passes for mainstream secular politics is also not very healthy. All too often, it has failed to question the orthodoxies of organized religions, be it Hinduism or Islam. Instead, with the instrumental logic of vote politics, it has often manipulated and stimulated all sorts of identities. No wonder, we are used to the classification of Brahmin votes, Dalit votes, Muslim votes. In its worst form, through a 'balancing' act, it has flirted with both majority communalism and minority communalism. And at its best, it has been reduced into mere symbolism: Machiavellian politicians with their dramaturgical performances celebrating Iftar parties! Meanwhile, the life-conditions of the minorities (as well as the other marginalized groups) remain dismal.

There is yet another issue. Our secular intellectuals have not really succeeded in establishing a spirit of communion with ordinary people. In fact, many of them—English-speaking, urban intellectuals well-versed in the discourses of Karl Marx and René Descartes—fail to understand even folk religiosity. Well, occasionally they might refer to Kabir and Surdas, celebrate sufi music, or sing Baul songs, but this, far from being authentic, is just a politically correct statement. It doesn't work. It doesn't heal. But I refuse to lose hope. Possibly, we will pass through this darkness, and welcome a new dawn with our awakened intelligence, spiritual awakening, compassionate listening and egalitarian spirit.

Avijit Pathak is a professor of Sociology at JNU.

From Secular to 'Sickular'

Mohammed Danish Iqbal

Secularism has become a source of deep schism in Indian society. Few terms trigger so much passion on either side of the aisle as secularism does. The nation today stands polarized between those who believe secularism alone can hold together a society as culturally and religiously diverse as India on the one hand, and those who denounce it as a foreign import imposed on a deeply religious society to appease the minorities, notably Muslims, on the other. Secular parties, particularly the Congress party, are accused of using secularism to garner Muslim/minority votes.

Supporters of secularism have become targets of hate and ridicule. The upsurge of the populist Right-wing politics has given a new edge to the anti-secularism mood. India's claim to be a secular democracy has rarely seemed more fragile. Secularism emerged as a necessary virtue for a stable social life amid the sectarian conflicts in the sixteenth-century Europe. Notwithstanding the complexities involved, the insulation of the state from religious perversions gradually became the cornerstone of liberal polity, espousing the cherished principles of tolerance, rationality, equality, etc. However, its journey to the traditionally religious societies, such as India, has been marked with social strife, anxiety and, of late, violence.

Even at the time of Independence, questions were raised about its suitability despite the robust endorsement it received from the leading political, social and religious figures of the national movement as the panacea for a peaceful co-existence among deeply religious communities. It was seen as a challenge to social sensibilities. Right-wing political organizations exploited this to their advantage, calling it pseudo-secularism.

This meant there always remained a camp that was deeply skeptical of its acceptability, and generally speaking, its appropriateness in Indian conditions. In the context of the nervous '80s and the near-complete breakdown that India witnessed in the '90s, particularly with the Shah Bano case and destruction of the Babri Masjid, secularism received its most trenchant scrutiny. It was variously seen as the construct of a 'modernist minority'—at odds with the real experience of ordinary Indians, both Hindus and Muslims.

Meanwhile, the issue of communalism is no longer about religious differences, but has transformed into a clash between majoritarian/national Hindu 'identity' and the Muslim 'identity'. And it is not just about being a Muslim, but what it *might mean* to be a Muslim. Therefore, anyone who is presumed to be a Muslim is deemed a fit target. Anyone with a Muslim name is regarded as the 'other'. Secularism started its journey underlying the principle of reason and justice, but is now mocked as 'sickular'. There is a lot to unpack as to how this has happened. The role of the media in spreading misinformation has been particularly disappointing. The future of Muslims is tied to the fate of secularism in India, and will greatly depend on how the majority community acts in future.

Mohammed Danish Iqbal is an assistant professor of English at AMU.

Muslims and Secularism

Mohammad Reyaz

At the height of the 2019 anti-CAA protests, began a side-debate that shaped not only the nature of the protests but also their direction. And this is how it happened.

Students at Delhi's JMI, the second best-known protest site after Shaheen Bagh, were heard chanting, *'Tera mera rishta kya, la ilahe illallah* [What is the relationship between you and me—our faith and belief in Almighty Allah] and 'Allahu Akbar'. This was seized by the ruling BJP and Hindutva trolls to discredit the movement. Even liberal Hindus were quick to react to what they saw as a sign that the protests were being hijacked by fundamentalists sparking calls for Muslims to keep the movement 'secular' if they wanted cross-community support, especially from the majority community. This led to a sudden and unseemly change of tactics: not only were suspected 'fundamentalists' got rid of, but in a desperate effort to demonstrate their secular credentials, the organizers went to the other extreme—resorting to performing hawan and reciting Gurubani, along with the Quran.

This was, of course, not the first time that Muslims had found themselves in such a situation. The pressure on Muslims to prove their loyalty to India at every turn is an old story with any hint of Muslimness being construed as a sign of disloyalty. The question is 'why'? Is it because of the way modern India has been imagined—an India where Muslims and Islam are seen as alien to its cultural ethos? Consequently, when a Muslim is seen as liberal or one sacrificing for his watan (nation), it is *despite* him being a Muslim, not *because* he is a Muslim and *hubbul-watani* (love for the nation) is part of his core beliefs. The Muslim assertion of their religious identity in public is deemed unsecular even by liberal-secular Muslims, mostly a westernized and agnostic metropolitan elite.

Lately, every few weeks, some celebrity Muslim author, actor, activist or influencer laments how they 'miss the India' where they used to join in for garhbha, and celebrate Diwali and Ramleela, or have inter-faith marriages. They lament at the apparent loss of India 'where I and what I was, was my only identity...(and) nobody bothered about my caste, sect, or religion'.[4] Many who express dismay over a resurgent aggressive Hindu nationalism are also concerned about the 'rise of extremism' among Muslim youth. While it is debatable if such a 'Ram Rajya' or utopian India ever existed, what this nostalgia for the past suggests is that once India was relatively syncretic, pluralistic and inclusive—encapsulated in the idea of the so-called Ganga–Jamuni tehzeeb. An India that has changed in the wake of Modi's 'new India'.

---

[4]@iamrana. Twitter, 18 November 2020, 6. 11 p.m., https://bit.ly/3HRilZ0. Accessed on 3 March 2022.

But I question the very fundamental basis of the Ganga–Jamuni tehzeeb that supposedly led to the flowering of the syncretic, inclusive, pluralistic culture. The Ganga–Jamuni tehzeeb grew in a milieu where the grand narrative, or the dominant culture of the ruling class was largely Islamicate—that is, a culture influenced by Islam though not entirely Islamic. Its openness allowed it to expand and accommodate varied and pluralistic traditions of the Indian subcontinent producing a popular culture that came to be known as Ganga–Jamuni tehzeeb or Hindustani traditions.

I dispute the general understanding of the Ganga–Jamuni tehzeeb, believed to be the bedrock of the Indian version of secularism, where most scholars presuppose the larger openness of Hindu/Indian culture. The fact, on the contrary, is that the language and grammar of the Ganga–Jamuni tehzeeb remained broadly Islamciate, accommodating different and often inherently contradicting strands. So deep was the influence of this syncretic culture that even when the rulers were Hindus, Islamicate traditions prevailed. Its decline started in the wake of the divide-and-rule policy of British colonialists. Not content with creating a rift between Hindus and Muslims, they created a new narrative which presented Muslims as outsiders, invaders and destroyers of Indian traditions. It made Islam the antithesis of everything that was good about India and, at the same time, conjured up an image of supremacist Hinduism.

Once this narrative was accepted and streamlined (advocated not only by Hindutva forces but also by liberal Hindu historians and intellectuals albeit in more sophisticated language, for example, Shashi Tharoor, in his book, *Why I Am a Hindu*), it was only a matter of time before the Ganga–Jamuni tehzeeb started to crumble deepening the Hindu–Muslim divide and ultimately ending up in the partition of the country whose shadow still hangs heavily on their relations. The failure of liberals in conceptualizing secularism has been compounded by a deep-seated prejudice towards Islam, thus distorting their view of Muslims, routinely dubbed as fundamentalists and extremists. For a way out of this impasse, first we will need to confront the chequered history of Hindu-Muslim relations and then reimagine secularism in the light of our experience so far. This demands a willingness to be truly inclusive and pluralistic, where everyone is treated as an equal citizen, irrespective of caste, faith, or gender as enshrined in the Constitution, and where there is no room for majoritarianism.

Mohammad Reyaz is an assistant professor at Department of Journalism and Mass Communication, Aliah University.

Blighted by Cultural Tribalism

Bilal Khan

A debate on the idea and meaning of secularism is raging in India. The Constitution emphasizes equality, freedom, democratic ideas and secularism, but 75 years after Independence, these remain an aspiration while identity politics and divisions along caste and religious lines continue to dominate our political discourse. Attempts to bring together a culturally diverse society around the idea of common and shared citizenship have been frustrated by votaries of populist nationalism and sectarian groups seeking to divide voters along communal and caste identities.

Ideas of secularism and cultural diversity as something to celebrate have been usurped by a culture of tribalism which divides people between 'us' and 'them', with those not like 'us' portrayed as enemies. Thus, even inter-caste and inter-religious marriages are not simply frowned upon, but there are now laws effectively criminalizing such cultural communions. Much of it goes down to historical, religious and cultural prejudices. Instead of going forward and rise above those old prejudices, we seem to be regressing. Much of the sentiments against Muslims and other minorities is due to a lack of exposure to each other's cultures. This ignorance is exploited by vested interests on both sides and exacerbated by a media, especially the electronic media, more interested in sensational headlines to attract more viewers than in facilitating a constructive dialogue. In order to move forward, we need to acknowledge and address these issues. There is a massive potential for peaceful co-existence, but sadly the political will is lacking. And, to be honest, I don't see things changing any time soon.

Bilal Khan is an architect based in Delhi.

The Problem With Indian Secularism

Mohammad Alfaz Ali

This is, perhaps, not the best time to defend the idea of secularism, but in its moment of crisis it would be apt to take a good hard look at it, and analyse it in the light of the context in which it emerged in India. While in Europe it emerged as a counter to the Church–State nexus—to draw a line between religion and the state—and in India, we adopted it as a means to ensure equality of all religions. It must be borne in mind that the anti-thesis of secularism is not communalism, but majoritarianism, and it was to avert the risk of majoritarianism that the founders of Indian constitution chose secularism—to preserve the pluralistic essence of India.

The risk of a Hindu-majority India turning against religious minorities was not merely theoretical. It was very real, and has very nearly come to fruition. As far back as 1923, the Hindu Mahasabha leader V.D. Savarkar coined the term Hindutva to represent a collective 'Hindu' identity as an essence of India. He envisaged a Hindu Rashtra in which non-Hindus would have to live as second-class citizens. In relation to Muslims, it was underpinned by the 'two-nation' theory later picked up by Mohammed Ali Jinnah to demand a separate Muslim homeland arguing that Muslims would not get equal treatment in a Hindu-majority India. Both

Savarkar and Jinnah believed that Hindus and Muslims represented two 'nations' with distinct and irreconcilable religious and cultural identities. It was in this context—to debunk the two-nation theory and to assure minorities that their rights would be protected in an independent India— that secularism was chosen as an antidote to the threat from majoritarianism.

But clearly, it has not succeeded in checking the rise of majoritarian tendencies, as is evident from attempts to decide questions of citizenship on the basis of religion through laws such as the controversial new citizenship act, the CAA, which singles out only persecuted Hindus in other countries for the right to claim Indian citizenship, while specifically barring Muslims from doing so. Likewise, laws being enacted by BJP-ruled states in the name of 'love jihad' and targeting Muslims, and the manner in which the ban on cow slaughter is being sought to be enforced point to a form of creeping majoritarianism.

Many reasons are offered for why secularism has not worked—one of them being the fact that it has come to be defined mostly in terms of Hindu–Muslim relations (Hindu nationalists see it as a form of Muslim 'appeasement') rather than being treated simply as a neutral organizing principle designed to avoid religious or cultural conflict by conferring equal rights on Indians irrespective of their faith or cultural creed.

The way forward lies in Muslims and other minority

groups getting politically more involved in mainstream politics around cross-community and secular issues—jobs, housing, individual rights, tolerance, free speech—and assert their rights as Indian citizens invoking the Indian constitution and their Indian heritage. The 2019–20 Shaheen Bagh protests against the CAA are a good example of secular political activism. Ultimately, politics matters because it is the only route to empowerment. The biggest challenge for Muslims and Muslim political parties is to avoid sectarianism and be inclusive—and yet be able to articulate their community's concerns without being labelled anti-secular.

Mohammad Alfaz Ali is a political researcher.

The Legacy of Shaheen Bagh

Sohail Hashmi

The Shaheen Bagh protests had several remarkable features which are unprecedented in the history of mass mobilization in independent India. In fact, some features of this agitation have no parallel in the entire history of mass mobilization in India. It was, perhaps, the first time that Muslims came out, as Muslims, in defence of a secular right, the right to citizenship based on birth and domicile. They took to the streets, holding up the Constitution and the Tricolour; they came out on their own, consciously working towards building a broader inclusive solidarity. They were not mobilized or led by the 'Muslim leadership'.

In fact, the so-called 'Muslim leadership' was nowhere in the leadership of this movement. On the other hand, those belonging to the traditional Muslim leadership—the Islamic clergy and politicians—desperately tried to catch up with the movement lest they would be left behind. The other, equally, if not more, important feature of this movement was the role of the Muslim women. No matter who thought of this method of protest, it was an inspiration, a kind of inspiration that strikes but rarely. There isn't a single instance of this kind of satyagraha in independent India and the unnamed woman or women who thought of this need to be recognized as inspirational leaders, the kind that is increasingly becoming a rarity in India.

In a marked, gender-role reversal, men played second fiddle to women, arranging supplies, raising funds, dropping and picking up kids from school and running a whole load of errands that are traditionally the preserve of women. The confidence with which these women faced the camera and explained in clear-cut terms the reasons for their protest came as an eye-opener to many among the entrenched elite who had subconsciously internalized the image of the oppressed, inarticulate, insecure, burkha-clad, helpless Muslim woman. Their articulation and confidence came from a far broader political and social awareness among ordinary Muslims. Perhaps its most innovative aspect was the reading of the Preamble of the Constitution as an oath and the simultaneous raising of two slogans, '*Inquilab Zindabad*', associated with the Left, (coined by Maulana Hasrat Mohani and popularized by Bhagat Singh) and '*Jai Bhim*' in the memory of Dr B.R. Ambedkar, (chairman of the Constitution Drafting Committee and the most revered leader of Dalits). This was not a mere ritual. Speaker after speaker constantly reminded the audience that this was not the fight of Muslims alone, but of all the marginalized, all the poor and the underprivileged.

Indeed, its biggest legacy would be the possibility of greater cooperation among politically aware youth, cutting across the Muslim and Dalit divide, that could then develop into a wider progressive platform. Shaheen Bagh released democratic energies and the manner in which it mobilized the Muslims community on an inclusive, democratic and secular platform and the freedom, articulation, plus the confidence and self-respect that Muslim women gained through this movement are dividends that are going to be a major resource for future struggles. India will need all this energy because India has to fight its hardest battle yet—the battle against jingoism and bigotry.

Sohail Hashmi is a celebrated writer and filmmaker.

Postscript

Will the Phoenix Rise Again?

'Tomorrow, and tomorrow, and tomorrow,
Creeps in this petty pace from day to day,
To the last syllable of recorded time...'

—Shakespeare's *Macbeth*

We hear myriad interpretations of Indian secularism and its impact on Hindu–Muslim relations depending on where the narrator is coming from and the narrative they have been fed. As Orson Welles, the famous filmmaker, said, the story is all in the framing.

'If you want a happy ending that depends, of course, on where you stop your story. You could write a heart-warming tale of a shy country girl who struggles to find her feet in the big city until a prince sweeps her off her feet, or a tragic one about a girl who marries a prince, discovers that he is in love with somebody else and dies,' he said.[1]

The story of our secularism is a mixed bag. It's as much a 'heart-warming tale' of a newly independent and traumatized nation's vision of an inclusive and tolerant society, as it is a 'tragic one' about systemic attempts to undermine and ultimately destroy that vision.

It's the second—the tragic bit—that haunted me while writing this book: is this it, then? The end of the road for an idea of India that once represented hope and optimism and inspired generations of Indians to rise above sectarianism and narrow identity politics? I was reminded of progressive Urdu poet Moin Ahsan Jazbi's ghazal, 'Zindagi Hai To Basar Bhi Hogi', describing what it feels like at the end of a long and difficult journey that hasn't perhaps gone quite according to the plan: a sense of exhaustion, weighed down by '*gard-e-safar*' (dust accumulated in the course of the journey) and tormented by moments of sorrow and despair.[2]

So, what exactly went wrong with our national journey?

---

[1] Welles, Orson. *The Big Brass Ring*, Eyewear Publishing, London, 1991.
[2] The ghazal also includes the following lines: *Manzil-e-ishq pe yaad aayenge kuch rah ke gham, Mujh se lipti hui kuch gard-e-safar bhi hogi.* [When I reach my destination and look back, I may remember some things that brought me sorrow, I will also be covered in the dust accumulated from my journey.]

How did the transition from 'secularism' to 'sickularism' happen, and Indianness morph into majoritarianism without anyone ostensibly noticing it? How did we come to this? The answer is: to some degree, we were all complicit in messing it up—political leaders of all hues, Right-wing Hindu nationalists, Muslim leadership and the wider secular-liberal establishment. Even if inadvertently, we all contributed to undermining secularism either through ideological prejudice, political abuse, or sheer complacency in the face of a simmering backlash.

There's a liberal narrative that we were blindsided by a sudden resurgence of majoritarian nationalism. But the fact, as documented elsewhere in this volume, is that we could see it coming since as far back as the 1980s–90s starting with the Ram Mandir campaign. Signs of an ideological shift were all around us, and those leading the charge made no secret of their intentions. The Hindu Right can be accused of many things, but not of hiding its agenda. On the contrary it announced it from rooftops. L.K. Advani, Sangh Parivar's prima donna at the time, sneeringly dismissed Indian secularism as 'pseudo-secularism', and called upon Hindus to assert their 'Hindu pride'. The demolition of Babri Masjid was not carried out secretly in the dead of night but in broad daylight and on live TV.

Yet, the liberal-secular impulse was to dismiss it simply as an act of vandalism by a fanatical fringe, and an administrative failure. There was a lot of hand-wringing and angry rhetoric but no serious effort was made to understand the phenomenon behind it or to grasp the fact that the old idea of India was dying on its feet; for doing so would have been an implicit acknowledgement of failure.

We had further glimpses of the changing ideological discourse—most notably when the BJP-led government of Atal Behari Vajpayee (1998–2004) chose to look the other way when Gujarat erupted into anti-Muslim violence in 2002, following an attack on the Sabarmati Express at Godhra allegedly by a Muslim mob.

Vajpayee, who was widely hailed as the party's liberal public face, himself indulged in some rather provocative rhetoric after the train attack.[3] We also saw a chauvinistic display of Hindu 'pride' memorably encapsulated in the BJP's 'India Shining' boast on the back of economic liberalization. That boast had its comeuppance as millions of struggling Indians to whom economic reforms brought no benefit found it insulting and voted the BJP out of office in 2004. But the impulses underlying the idea of a 'new' majoritarian India survived.

Not only did it survive, but went on to gain more strength so that barely ten years later, it finally succeeded in toppling the old order—that, too, with a whopping popular mandate. Narendra Modi's 2014 electoral triumph

---

[3]Varadarajan, Siddharth. 'Let Us Not Forget the Glimpse We Got of the Real Vajpayee When the Mask Slipped', *TheWire*, 18 August 2018, https://bit.ly/3HAwVUP. Accessed on 28 February 2022.

represented an emphatic Hindu rejection of Nehruvian secularism. It shook the foundations of secular edifice to its roots. And if there were any lingering doubts, they were laid to rest with the BJP's subsequent election victories, and another emphatic general election win in 2019. The so-called secular parties were left reeling; if a general election was to be held 'tomorrow', the smart money would, again, be on Modi's idea of 'new' India.

Looking back, it seems extraordinary how quickly an idea that formed the ideological cornerstone of post-Independence modern India fell out of favour across large swathes of the political and intellectual spectrum. To the extent that many hitherto avowed secularists—academics, media commentators and social scientists—switched sides proudly 'confessing' that they had got it wrong the first time; and that secularism was indeed a foreign import imposed on the country by a Left-wing liberal elite to appease Muslims.

In an article in *The Hindu*, days after Modi's 2014 election victory, avowedly liberal social scientist Shiv Visvanathan approvingly quoted a colleague who told him, 'You English speaking secularists have been utterly coercive, making the majority feel ashamed of what was natural.'[4]

'The Left intellectuals and their liberal siblings behaved as a club, snobbish about secularism, treating religion not as a way of life but as a superstition... By overemphasising

---

[4]Visvanathan, Shiv. 'How Modi Defeated Liberals Like Me', *The Hindu*, 26 May 2016, https://bit.ly/3sB5y8R. Accessed on 28 February 2022.

secularism, they created an empty domain, a coercive milieu where ordinary people practising religion were seen as lesser orders of being,' he wrote, citing his colleague.[5] Narendra Modi, he argued, 'turned the tables by showing secularism...was a hypocrisy, or was becoming a staged unfairness which treated minority violations as superior to majoritarian prejudices.'[6] When I wrote a rejoinder, I was told by BJP supporters to go to Pakistan if I was not happy in India.

Ironically, even Muslims started questioning the idea—portraying their community as a 'hapless' victim of scheming secularists. By way of flavour, here's what Shahid Siddiqui, a relatively moderate Muslim leader and editor of *Nai Duniya*, wrote at the time echoing the BJP's attacks on secularism: 'How long are Indian Muslims going to be the slaves of this "electoral secularism", the sole purpose of which is to create fear in the minds of the minorities?'[7] Siddiqui, a former MP, associated with assorted secular groups, including the Congress, also put out a series of angry tweets denouncing secular 'saviours' of Muslims as their 'worst enemies'. He tweeted that Muslims had been 'pushed into socio-economic ghetto not by BJP but by Cong& [sic] SP'; and that 'Muslims r [sic] unable to see that they have become

---

[5]Ibid.
[6]Ibid.
[7]@shahid_Siddiqui. Twitter, 2 April 2014, 12:33 p.m., https://bit.ly/35TTG8K. Accessed on 3 March 2022.

slaves of secularism to suit a coterie ruling this country using Muslims as a vehicle to power'.[8]

A view, once confined to the fringes of the Right, started to spill into mainstream liberal intellectual discourse prompting some to liken the trend to a version of Stockholm syndrome'. An article in *The Hindu* argued: 'When the chips are down and morale is low it is easy to slip into a sort of Stockholm syndrome and start sympathising with the opponent's viewpoint.' It said the 2014 general election results (celebrated as a victory of Hindu nationalism over 'pseudo-secularism'), was 'having the same effect on some liberal voices'.[9]

To get a sense of the seismic transformation of the national mood, it's important to remember that India's secular democracy—and India's ability to hold a hugely diverse society together in the face of dire predictions—was one of the biggest success stories of twentieth century. It was looked upon as a beacon of hope in the rest of South Asia, rocked by political and social instability, not least in its immediate neighbourhood across the border in Pakistan.

Secularism tapped into our nobler instincts and made millions of Indians seek to live in peace and harmony after

---

[8]@shahid_siddiqui. Twitter, 25 March 2014, 5:17 a.m., https://bit.ly/3hNb4Ps. Accessed on 3 March 2022.
[9]Suroor, Hasan. 'Let's Debate Secularism, Not Rubbish It', *The Hindu*, 6 June 2014, https://bit.ly/3vwqMqg. Accessed on 28 February 2022.

a bloody Partition. It gave us a vision of an India proud of its religious and cultural diversity, an India in which every citizen, irrespective of their faith or ethnicity, would have equal rights. But, more importantly, at the time, secularism looked like the only common-sense option to heal the wounds of Partition and offer Muslims a sense of security in a Hindu-majority India. There was also a wider—somewhat politically opportunistic—consideration, as argued elsewhere in the book: an attempt to gain a moral high ground vis-à-vis Pakistan—a secular India versus a theocratic Islamic Pakistan.

Where it went wrong—and what secularists refuse to acknowledge—is how secularism was abused by secular parties, not least the Congress party. Its record on secularism is dire. It failed to protect minorities and, often, actually stoked sectarian violence, most infamously during the 1984 anti-Sikh riots. Even the demolition of the Babri Masjid, under the watch of the Congress party government, had its roots in its attempts to appease competing strains of Muslim and Hindu fundamentalism (Rajiv Gandhi had ordered for a part of the mosque to be opened up for Hindu worship, to deal with the criticism of his government's decision to overturn the Supreme Court verdict on the Shah Bano case granting an elderly divorcee the right to claim a maintenance allowance from her ex-husband) as discussed in previous chapters.

None of this, though, invalidates the profound importance of secularism in such a culturally diverse society as India.

It bears repetition that for all its flaws and bungled execution, secularism served its purpose at a time when the country was reeling from the aftermath of a communal bloodbath in the wake of Partition. It was a much-needed balm and the only civilized approach to bring the country together. And, it worked, even if in fits and starts and did not always satisfy everyone. If nothing else, we learned to tolerate—if, not exactly, respect—religious and cultural differences. Despite tensions, we got along. We managed to be civil to each other.

But the problem with sticking plasters—even the best of them—is that they are just that: sticking plasters can do only so much to alleviate a situation. They are not a substitute for a permanent fix. This is what happened with secularism. It worked admirably for a while in holding the nation together at a critical moment. However, it started to wear out in the absence of any serious effort or a coherent strategy to fix the deepening communal divide stoked by groups opposed to the idea that Muslims should enjoy equal status in Hindu-majority India. Its abuse by secular parties through unprincipled compromises with Muslim fundamentalists groups in the name of protecting Muslim 'identity' compounded the crisis. This led even moderate/secular Hindus to start questioning secularism, suggesting that it was simply a cover to appease Muslim voters. And, thanks to a little help from the Sangh Parivar, it didn't take long before this simmering resentment grew into a full-blown backlash. The rest, as the cliché goes, is history.

So, here we are in 2022, in what looks like a very different country from where we began 75 years ago. To quote historian Shruti Kapila, 'New and conservative India is the opposite and mirror image of national India that Nehru discovered, invented and owned.'[10]

As someone who never lost a chance to tick off my Pakistani and Middle Eastern friends for how they treat minorities in their countries, it pains me to hear the name of my own country being increasingly mentioned in the same breath as them. The joke now is on me as they gleefully tell me to 'join the club'.

But, there are many liberals I know and respect who continue to maintain that it's simply a passing phase, a 'bubble', as they call it, which will burst once people finally 'see through their real agenda'. It's clear that the real significance of the change in the national mood has still not fully sunk in.

The truth is that, like it or not, and regardless of the reasons, there's now a 'new' majoritarian India, and a refusal to acknowledge it will not make it go away. Not to put too fine a point on it, a Hindu India is already here in all but name.

According to political scientist Zoya Hasan, Modi's 2014 triumph was 'not just one party replacing the other

---

[10]Kapila, Shruti. 'Conservatism and the Cult of the Individual in a Populist Age', *Making Sense of Modi's India*, Hasan Suroor (ed.), HarperCollins, New Delhi, 2016.

but an indication of a clear shift in the ideological discourse of Indian politics'.[11]

'The idea of "majoritarianism" acquired political legitimacy for the first time,' she wrote, arguing that 'a large section of the electorate is not bothered about majoritarianism as long as it does not affect their personal domain and as long as the government succeeds in delivering higher economic growth and jobs'.[12]

Meanwhile, the meandering debate on Hindu–Muslim relations is going nowhere and has become so polarized that it's increasingly starting to sound like a dialogue of the deaf with nobody inclined to listen to the other side. Moreover, it has got bogged down in the larger argument over secularism. The liberals see secularism and the so-called 'Muslim question' as integral parts of a constitutional settlement that envisaged equal rights for all Indian citizens irrespective of their faith. They believe that any attempt to tinker with it would render this constitutional arrangement unfit and pave the way for 'communalists' to take over.

Framing Hindu–Muslim relations as a 'secularism vs communalism' issue was always risky because it allowed the so-called nationalists to call into question the very idea of secularism—a European concept smuggled in by a western-educated liberal elite and imposed on a historically religious society.

---

[11]Hasan, Zoya. 'Collapse of the Congress Party', *Rise of Saffron Power*, Mujibur Rehman (ed.), Routledge India, London, 2018.
[12]Ibid.

Ostensibly, the battle for secularism is meant to protect Muslim interests. But, in reality, it is hurting them as they find themselves uneasily caught up between maximalist liberals who insist that a constitutionally secular state alone can protect minority rights and aggressive Hindu nationalists who claim that an ancient civilization like India (home to people from different cultures for centuries) doesn't need an 'alien' ideology to teach it tolerance.

Apart from the nationalist rhetoric, the 'secularism-or-nothing' argument is problematic, in the very least, because it elevates faith above other, less-emotive elements of identity and brings back all the bad memories of Hindu–Muslim conflicts ignoring centuries-old shared cultural bonds. Recently, I got into an argument with an old (Hindu) friend on Facebook after he suggested that what was happening to Muslims in India today was simply a case of the empire striking back. Or as he put it: 'A natural but belated response to militant Islam and Christianity.'

After a few testy exchanges, however, he wrote: 'Allahu Akbar... *Jai Sri Ram*...Hindus and Muslims have a centuries-old shared heritage in India... In the coming years, the good old times will return. This is my prophecy.' I found his comment revealing as it showed that for all the Muslim-bashing, there's still a grudging acknowledgement of what he called the 'centuries-old shared heritage'. It's perhaps a minor nuance—often overlooked in today's polarized discourse—but it offers a glimmer of hope. I believe all is still not lost and we can yet find a way to bring some civility to Hindu–Muslim relations as a nod to this sense of 'shared heritage', however grudging and nebulous.

We may not be able to 'un-become what we have become' as a character in a play by British playwright Kwame Kwei-Armah says, but we can try and limit further damage. And that means a willingness to start looking for less contentious alternatives based around what binds us by virtue of common citizenship and shared history rather than what divides us. I believe that a common national culture can be the basis for a new Hindu–Muslim settlement placing cultural affinity above faith. And it's not just me.

A number of prominent liberal sociologists such as Neera Chandhoke and Rajeev Bhargava have called for a rethink on secularism in order to deal with a creeping 'post-secular' age. Constitutional scholar Faizan Mustafa has gone to the extent of advocating 'some kind of Hindu Rashtra' while guaranteeing 'substantial rights to minorities'.[13]

Admittedly, it's a controversial argument, but as I've argued throughout this book, the notion that only a self-avowed secular state is capable of protecting its minorities is a fallacy. A country can have a state religion and yet make no distinction between its citizens because of their race or religion. In another chapter, I've listed the countries,

---

[13]Mustafa, Faizan. 'Minorities, Too, Are Fed Up With This Façade of Secularism', *The Indian Express*, 21 March 2020, https://bit.ly/3MafQo4. Accessed on 24 February 2022.

including some Muslim states, which have a hybrid system: there's an official state religion, but in everyday practice, the government makes no distinction between its citizens on the basis of faith, colour or ethnicity.

Take my adopted country, the UK. Its official religion is Christianity; the House of Commons starts its sittings with a Christian prayer; and the Church of England is officially represented in the House of Lords by a group of bishops. But its policies are secular with all British citizens, regardless of their faith and ethnicity, guaranteed equal treatment. It's an excellent example of a faith-based secular state. It has a rigorously enforced equality law that makes discrimination an offence. Contrast this with India, where we have all the constitutional trappings of a secular state, but it offers little protection to minorities in practice.

What is preferable? A state secular on paper, but in effect practising religious apartheid, or a state with an official religion, but secular in practice—a sort of a secular Hindu state, for example?

Politically isolated and facing an existential crisis, the question before the Muslim community is whether it wants to prolong the agony and continue to suffer daily humiliation or try and find a dignified way out of it. There are no easy options: either we continue to be trapped in a no-man's land—nominally secular, but in practice discriminatory—waiting for Godot to deliver us from our misery; or swallow our ego, grind our teeth and give up the tottering ghost of secularism for good. It might seem like an extreme step, but in effect, we will be simply formalizing what's already a de facto situation.

Some will see this as 'surrender', but will actually allow us to bow out at a time of our own choosing rather than have a solution imposed on us, as happened in the case of Babri Masjid and triple talaq. In exchange, we can insist on constitutional and legal guarantees around the protection of Muslim rights as equal citizens of India.

Let's get this straight: there's no Godot coming to our rescue. Secularism and Muslims are considered lost causes and increasingly a political liability even by avowedly liberal mainstream parties. They're vying with each other to demonstrate their Hinduness—a sign that the Indian political landscape has changed for good. There's a new normal and as the English philosopher Alan Watts famously said, 'The only way to make sense of change is to plunge into it, move with it'. Which, in this case, means that we stop endlessly arguing about the past and, instead, move on. And try and make the best of a bad situation. It's easy to bury one's head in the sand and refuse to acknowledge the reality, but it requires courage to confront it and deal with it.

Jazbi's ghazal ends on an optimistic note suggesting that a new dawn follows every dark night—'s*haam aayee hai to aaye ke sehar bhi hogi*'. I wish I could share his optimism, but hey, who knows. The myth of the phoenix rising from the ashes is still very much alive.

Addenda

Rethinking Secularism

Rajeev Bhargava

The secular state is besieged in India. But it is a mistake to think that the siege began with the coming to power of the new government, though it can't be denied that forces have been unleashed more recently that attack the secular ethos of our society in a manner that is more blatant, persistent, frontally direct and shamelessly open. However, wittingly or unwittingly, deliberately or unintentionally, various groups in our society have been chipping away at the secular edifice, so that gradually, overtime, its moral legitimacy has been eroded. To put it differently, although secularism has long been facing an external threat by those who vigorously oppose it and this challenge has been political, social, cultural and intellectual, secularism has also been facing an internal threat in the sense that, the myopia, neglect, complacency, propensity for ritual hyperbole, weakness of will or failure of nerve of its proponents has also undermined it. This internal threat has also been political, social, cultural and intellectual.

My focus today is on such internal, intellectual factors that have led to the moral delegitimization of secularism. More specifically, I speak of the conceptual flaws in the understanding and defence of secularism. It is important to point out that I do not believe that internal, intellectual reasons contributed more to the crisis of secularism. Far from that. Indeed, their role may be less significant than external, non-intellectual factors. But internal factors are more in our control; we can do something immediately about them. Besides, I don't think secularism can be rescued without some course correction which in turn is impossible without self-reflexivity and self-criticism.

Meaning of Secularism

Those who defend secularism have frequently lost sight of the whole point behind a secular state, what secularism is for. More specifically, they do not fully understand what it was that gave Indian secularism its point and what made it distinctive, even unique. To elaborate this issue, allow me to furnish some examples: a woman is burnt at the stake because she is believed to be a witch; a man is stoned to death for heresy; a woman is not allowed to enter a temple because she is more than 15 and less than 55 years old, a time span in which she is menstruating and hence 'polluted'; a man from the lowest caste, believed to be an untouchable is not allowed to take water from the well.

What is common to all these examples? In all these cases, (a) some person is discriminated against, excluded, marginalized, intimidated, oppressed or humiliated on grounds of religion or somewhere along the chain of reasoning behind it, a religious rationale is cited. (b) In each of these cases, both the victim and the perpetrator are from the same religious community. Call this intra-religious domination. Intra-religious domination takes other forms too as when (a) Ahemdias are deemed to be non-Muslims and their places of worship prevented from being called 'mosques', (b) when Catholics are persecuted by Lutherans or (c) a Shaivite temple is desecrated by Vaishaivites.

Take another set of examples. A tax is imposed on Hindus but not on Muslims; Churches are attacked by intolerant Hindus or militant Muslims; Catholic schools are subsidized by the state but Hindu, Muslim, Protestant and Jewish schools are not; a person called Hussain is unable to get a house on rent in metropolitan cities. Here again we have (a) discrimination, exclusion, marginalization, oppression or humiliation on grounds of religion but (b) victims and perpetrators come from different religious communities. Call this inter-religious domination.

The point I wish to make through these examples is that Secularism must be seen as a critical social perspective not against every religious formation, or against religiosity or religion per say but against all forms of institutionalized religious domination. Political Secularism is a narrower perspective, according to which a state should be so designed as to reduce institutionalized religious domination in both its forms, inter- and intra-religious. Its main claim is that if institutionalized religious domination is to be reduced, then states should not be captured by or align themselves with a particular religious community or a section thereof. Some form of separation between state and institutionalized religion is necessary.

Now this idea that secularism is not anti-religious but against different forms of institutionalized religious domination was novel, a conception that was invented under very special circumstances that had emerged in India specific conditions in India before and at the time of its independence from colonial rule.

Majority-Minority Syndrome

The story of what happened in the first half of the twentieth century in India is familiar to all of us but it is still worth recalling. Sections of Hindu and Muslim elites had at that time been sucked into what can be called a majority-minority syndrome... It is a feature of this syndrome that, groups make demands on one other that can rarely be fulfilled, conjure up imaginary grievances, insist precisely on that which hurts the other most, at one time obsessively desires the very same thing that the other wants, at another time the exact opposite, always with the sole purpose of negating the claims of the other. In this condition animosity between groups circulates freely, adding layer upon layer of grievances and antagonistic games are played with no end in mind except the defeat and humiliation of the other. Ambedkar provides several examples: 'Hindus and Muslims make preparations against each other', he tells us, 'without abatement reminding one of a 'race in armaments between two hostile nations. If the Hindus have the Banaras University, the Musalmans must have the Aligarh University. If the Hindu start *Shuddhi* movement, the Muslims must launch the *Tablig* movement. If the Hindus start sangathan, the Muslims must have the *Tanjim*. If the Hindus have the RSS, the Muslims must reply by organising the *Khaksars*'. A group of Muslims had psyched themselves into a state of paranoia that was only partly grounded in fears of inter-religious domination but which got exacerbated and became a very real prospect after the formation of Pakistan.

But a majority-minority syndrome had another consequence. In the 19th century, a number of freedom- and equality-centred reform movements had been initiated within Hindus and Muslims. But a majority-minority syndrome set off by inter-communal rivalry forestalled these reforms, intensifying anti-reformist tendencies... It was in such a context replete with continuing inter- and intra-religious domination that independent India had to decide the character of the newly instituted state and its relationship with religion. It had two options: either to have a majoritarian religion-centered state that consolidates both forms of inter-religious domination, a patriarchal, upper-caste dominated Hindu majoritarian state or a state that contains these tendencies and tries to reduce both these forms of domination. In 1950, when India was declared a republic, it chose to have a secular state *despite* the massacre and displacement of millions of people on ethno-religious grounds, not to offer 'a final solution' by expulsion or liquidation of all but the dominant religious group but with the explicit objective of dealing with tensions generated continuously by deep religious diversity. In doing so they developed a distinctive conception of secularism.

Why is this secularism distinctive? Because unlike say the French or Turkish model, it was not anti-religious. In the French state, for example, (a) religion is not officially recognized, (b) it becomes a target of active disrespect by a state that excludes religion from its affairs but retains the power to intervene in religion, (c) is removed from the public domain i.e. privatized, (d) qualification of citizenship, both membership in the state and all rights are made wholly independent of religious affiliation. As I shall explain below, Indian secularism is very different. Likewise, it is also unlike the American model in which (a) the non-recognition of religion is accompanied by a different understanding of what separation means. Here, religion and state are mutually excluded from each other—none has the right or the power to intervene in the affairs of one another. Thus, the state has no power to intervene in religious affairs... All 'western' states grew out of the need to respond to challenge posed to individuals and non-religious groups by a politically meddlesome and socially oppressive church in a context of virtual religious homogeneity.

In India on the other hand, (a) a distinction is drawn between the identity of the state which is made entirely independent of religion and an important but limited sphere where religion is officially recognized (Articles 25-30 in the Indian Constitution). (b) The state is required to be equally (well- or ill-) disposed to all religions. No religion is supposed to be politically dominant or favoured by the state. The state is meant to challenge not support inter-religious domination. (c) Religion is understood to be a complex, morally ambiguous phenomenon—some aspects of which require negative state intervention—ban on untouchability, the order that all temples be opened to all sections of Hindus, the law that seeks to keep religious restrictions away from the exercise of basic individual rights of women—(state against intra-religious domination), some aspects require positive intervention—exemption to Sikhs from wearing standard headgear in the army or the police, and still other aspects that require that the state keep entirely away from religion, a space must exist where religious individuals and communities are entirely free to do as they believe are required by their religion. (d) There is no blanket disrespect towards religions nor an unqualified respect for them but an rather an attitude of critical respect. (e) Unlike both the French and American models, state is not strictly separated from religion. Instead the state keeps a policy of principled distance from all religions and (f) the qualification for citizenship qua membership in the state is made wholly independent of religious affiliation and although most rights are independent of religion, some are dependent on membership in religious communities...

Flawed Defence

Most Indian secularists have frequently defended not this complex, sophisticated, very Indian model but instead some very limited and partial version of it or worse, one or the other western variants. They have alternatingly defended a secularism that is anti-religious—alienating the religious by failing to treat them as citizens worthy of equal respect—sometimes put their force behind an areligious secularism—failing to understand that no modern state can keep itself aloof from religion, especially in places like India where religion cannot easily be separated from the social and the cultural, and sometimes chosen to support a multi-religious secularism that has a high propensity to tolerate indefensible socio-religious practices and that cries foul every time the state intervenes in religion. This has got defenders of secularism into a mess. They have intervened in religion when they should not have, intervened when restraint was desperately needed and frequently continued to respect aspects of religion not worthy of respect and disrespect those facets that deserved respect. An acute understanding of the complex and variegated ways in which inter- and intra-religious domination persists in the interstices of Indian society has been elusive and therefore has been challenged, if at all, only half-heartedly.

One manifestation of this misunderstanding is the complete and exhaustive identification of secularism with a defence of minority rights, as if the only purpose of secularism is to equally respect all religions and to provide support to all of them my third proposition. On this view, fighting inter-religious domination seems to be the only raison d'etre of secularism. But this forgets that an equally important purpose of Indian secularism and indeed the primary purpose of all western secularisms has been to counter intra-religious domination. That one function of a secular state is to encourage freedom, equality and justice-centred reforms in every religion, to protect individuals from oppression by their own fellow co-religionists, indeed, to rescue ordinary Hindus, Muslims, Christians and Sikhs from their own religious extremists, to liberate religion from bigotry and fanaticism, simply slips off the radar of secularism. The marginalization of socio-religious reform in the agenda of Indian secularism and the resulting exclusive focus on minority rights lends credence to the mostly unjust charge of minorityism. If secularism is seen as concerned solely with the defence of minority rights, it can be viewed as a tool to protect the interests of Muslims and Christians, and having little to do with Hindus. It can then be twisted to appear as pro-Muslim and anti-Hindu. But secularism is needed as much to protect Hindus from their own extremists and homogenizers and from the exclusionary instincts of its traditional power wielders that have cared little in the past for Dalits and women.

Put differently, the reduction of secularism to a minority-protection device and the disconnection of minority-rights discourse from feminist and Dalit discourses has led to the weakening of the politics of all vulnerable sections of society. Instead of standing together and complementing one another, today, secular, feminist and Dalit discourses in many contexts, confront one another as competitors, if not opponents. The strength of Indian secularism—its defence of minority rights—is easily made to appear as its weakness and the burden of its defence, rather than be shared by all citizens, falls on the minorities and 'pro-minority' secularists. This is both unfair and unnecessary...

Misunderstanding Secularism

The misunderstanding of Indian secularism, especially as an anti-religious doctrine, has meant that secularists have not maintained a proper distinction between the communitarian and the communal. A communitarian position is one that an individual is at least partly defined by his or her religious/philosophical commitments and traditions (community) and therefore that there is nothing inappropriate in proclaiming that one is a Hindu/Muslim/Sikh/Christian/Marxist/Advaita and so on. Indeed, in some instances, a person may even take legitimate pride in one's community and community identity—as long as the person is also prepared to be openly ashamed when there is good reason to. A communitarian position is different from a communal one. A communal perspective is one in which one's community identity is defined in opposition to, not in dialogue with, other communities... such that the existence and interests is necessarily viewed as being at the expense of other communities and community identities. It is communal to believe or act in a way that presupposes that one can't be a Hindu without being anti-Muslim or vice-versa. Communalism is communitarianism gone sour... The conflation of communitarian and communal in India has often meant that secular persons with a Hindu background or identity have not found a way of articulating the religious or socio-religious interests of Hindus without sounding communal and have often appeared to have defended Muslim faith and interests in bad faith, as if in doing so, they were really being communal but this was permissible given the vulnerability of minorities in a representative democracy dominated by Hindus. The fact is that there is nothing wrong in articulating and defending some Hindu, Muslim and Christian interests when they do not come into conflict with one another. This can be done without guilt or shame. However, sadly, Indian secularism has rarely sorted out this issue and dispelled this confusion. Lack of clarity and honesty has bred indefensible swings from one communal position to another and a lot of avoidable hypocrisy. Proponents of secularism have managed to avoid this problem occasionally, sporadically, inconsistently, somewhat superficially and half-heartedly but had to and will have to do so with greater understanding of each other's religious tradition, consistently, all the time... Defenders of secularism need to do three things simultaneously and consistently. Their defence of minority rights must always be accompanied by a robust critique of minority extremism and all forms of communalisms and both of these must always reflect a deeper understanding, and defence of the best of every religious tradition. Our critiques of minority extremism and majoritarianism must reflect that we know minority and majority religious traditions from the inside.

Edited excerpts from the 16th Ashgar Ali Engineer Memorial Lecture, 'Does Indian Secularism Have a Future?', September 2020. It drew on a lecture he delivered in Mumbai in 2014 and later published in *Secularism Under Siege: Revisiting the Indian Secular State* (edited by Zaheer Ali), 2015. Reproduced with the author's permission.

Minorities, Too, Are Fed Up With This Façade Of Secularism

Faizan Mustafa

Secularism demonstrates modernity and remains the best option for any progressive nation. Is it not a fact that it made us a global power and Pakistan a failed state? Nepal saw merit in it and has become a secular state. But if Hindus really feel threatened from Muslims and Christians, we must address their concerns and not shy away from discussing the possibility of a Hindu Rashtra. Minorities, too, are now fed up with this façade of secularism, with all state institutions tilting towards one religion. Perhaps some kind of Hindu Rashtra can help us bring peace and save the country from the path of self-destruction.

We have several models from modern democracies to choose from, such as the Christian states of England, Ireland, and Greece, the Jewish state of Israel, Muslim states like Pakistan and Bangladesh and the Buddhist state of Sri Lanka. A Hindu Rashtra will certainly sound the death knell of the idea of India that celebrated diversity and will lower our international standing, but minorities should not worry too much about it. Just like several other modern theocracies, a Hindu Rashtra could guarantee substantial rights to religious minorities. It will not be based on the Manusmriti and will uphold modern ideas of human rights, particularly the right to equality and non-discrimination.

A Secular Hindu Rashtra?

Many experts have been writing that since India has not seen religious wars and the Church–State conflict, secularism was an alien concept. Indians are essentially religious and, therefore, the wall that separates the state and church is inappropriate for us. In fact, that's why Indian secularism talks of equal respect for all religions. There are two models of secularism—the non-establishment or the separation of the Church and State model (USA, France) that India adopted and the jurisdiction model of England, Ireland and Greece. Nehruvian secularism intended to achieve the former. Under the separation model, the state and church are expected to be hostile to each other but in the jurisdiction model, the two may co-exist—therefore, it is possible to have a Hindu Rashtra even under the secular model.

Since we are dissatisfied with the separation model, the European jurisdiction model could be our first option, if we want to become a Hindu Rashtra. The Anglican Church is the official Church of England and the queen is the defender of faith. We, too, may declare Hinduism to be the official religion of the state and, like England, give equal rights to all citizens ensuring freedom of religion and prohibiting discrimination on the basis of religion.

The Irish Constitution offers another model. The

preamble begins with the name of the most holy trinity. But the state cannot endow any religion or discriminate on religious grounds... (Likewise) Article 3 of the Greek Constitution declares the Greek orthodox church as the 'dominant religion'. The opening words of the preamble are—'In the name of Holy, Consubstantial and Undivided Trinity'. Article 33 requires that the President and MPs shall take oath in the name of Holy Trinity. But, Article 4 talks of the right to equality. Article 5(2) guarantees right to life, liberty and honour without any discrimination on the basis of religion and accords freedom of religion to all faiths...

Israel does not have a written Constitution. But its basic law guarantees human dignity, liberty, equality and freedom of religion. The Jewish Democratic state has an arrangement to unite the synagogue with the state. In its original form, Zionism was all about civic nationalism. By the 1970s, Israeli identity was converted into Jewish identity. Interestingly, it has achieved secularisation without secularism. It gives a number of rights to its minorities. All religious groups have their own religious laws and courts. Arabic is the second state language. In fact, Sharia courts have more powers than Jewish, Christian and Druze courts and their decisions are executed like verdicts of civil courts. Arabs are mentioned as Arab-Israeli citizens.

Best Options

Bangladesh and Sri Lanka are much better options. Even though secularism was one of the fundamental principles of Bangladesh's original constitution, it was deleted in 1977 by General Ziaur Rahman. Islam was declared the state religion in 1988. But in 2010, the Supreme Court of Bangladesh restored secularism as one of the basic features of the Constitution. In 2011, the Constitution was amended and the term 'secular' was reinserted.

Though Article 9 of the Sri Lankan Constitution falls short of declaring Buddhism as the state religion, it does give 'Buddhism' the 'foremost place' and puts an obligation on the state to protect and foster, 'Buddha Sasana'. It not only guarantees freedom of religion, but, unlike India, Article 10 gives 'freedom to have or adopt a religion or belief of his choice'. Minorities are governed by their personal laws and sharia courts function within the premises of regular courts.

If we are really fed up with the separation model of secularism and want to adopt the jurisdiction model with India being declared a Hindu Rashtra or giving Hinduism the status of dominant spiritual heritage, we must ensure that it brings with it genuine liberalism, substantive equality, modernity and, above all, state responsibility towards religious minorities with the guarantee of freedom and cultural autonomy. If even this cannot bring to an end the project of hate and polarization, we have no option but to strengthen our original concept of secularism and work towards the emancipation of state from religion. (ends)

Excerpts from an article published in *The Indian Express*, 21 March 2020. Reproduced, courtesy of the author who is the vice chancellor, NALSAR University of Law, Hyderabad.

… *Addenda* ♦ 175

Secularism in the Constituent Assembly Debates, 1946–1950

Shefali Jha

Secularism, it has been argued, failed to stem the spread of communalism in India, because its marginalising and contempt of religion bred a backlash on which communalism thrived. This article contends that this 'contempt for religion' was marginalised in the course of the secularism debates in the Constituent Assembly. The dominant position on secularism that a 'democratic' Constitution find place for religion as a way of life for most Indians triumphed over those who wished for the Assembly to grant only a narrow right to religious freedom, or to make the uniform civil code a fundamental right. These early discussions on religious freedom also highlight a paradox—it is precisely some of the advocates of a broad right to religious freedom who were also the most vociferous opponents of any political rights for religious minorities.

The Preamble and Conceptions of Secularism

When the preamble to the Constitution was discussed in the Constituent Assembly on October 17, 1949, disagreement and acrimonious debate over the incorporation of the principle of secularism took up most of the Assembly's time. The positions spelt out on secularism on that day show up clearly the lines of difference that had been developing on this issue during the three years of the Constituent Assembly debates... The preamble was discussed in one of the last sessions of the Constituent Assembly which is why the theoretical positions on secularism that we try to extrapolate from the...debate reflect the stands taken during the preceding three years. All the members agreed, of course, on the necessity of establishing a secular state. Most shared an understanding of history in which the 'movement for the separation of religion and state was irrevocably a part of the project for the democratisation of the latter'. How could a democratic state represent a religious majority at the expense of the rights and liberties of a minority? In Europe, 'the idea of democratic dissent was posed initially as the idea of religious difference. It gradually became the premise for the liberties of the individual in general, and, in raising the question of equality and equal rights for all, the idea of secularism became the chief motor behind the subsequent idea of political democracy'.[1] Since independent India was to be a democracy, secularism was a fait accompli: 'it is essential for the proper functioning of democracy that communalism should be eliminated from Indian life'.[2] But the question remained as to the kind of secularism to be

---

[1] Ahmad, Aijaz. *Lineages of the Present*, Tulika, New Delhi. 1996, p. 313.
[2] Rao, B. Shiva. *The Framing of India's Constitution: Select Documents—Vol. IV*, Government of India Press, Nasik, 1968, p. 593.

established by Indians faced with the problem of 'creating a secular state in a religious society'.

Was a state secular only when it stayed strictly away from religion, and could such a secular state survive only if society was slowly secularised as well? Or did a state that equally respected all religions best capture the meaning of secularism in the Indian context? On this issue we can see three alternative positions in the controversy around the preamble. The first—which we call the no-concern theory of secularism—saw a definite line of separation between religion and the state. Given the principles of freedom of expression and religious liberty, it was up to the individual to decide whether to be a believer or not, or to adhere to this religion or that. Therefore the preamble could not contain any references to god, and neither should the constitution establish links between the state and any religion. This argument of religion being an individual's private affair, was extended during the main sessions of the Constituent Assembly to include the more radical claim that religion must be relegated to the private sphere. Many members declared that the need of the hour was to strengthen the identity of Indians as citizens of the Indian state, as opposed to being members of some community or religious group. Radhakrishnan's speech on the Objectives Resolution on December 13, 1946 asserted that 'nationalism, not religion, is the basis of modern life...the days of religious states are over. These are the days of nationalism'.[3] A month later, G.B. Pant, speaking to the Advisory Committee of the Constituent Assembly proclaimed that the 'individual citizen who is really the backbone of the state...has been lost here in that indiscriminate body known as the community. We have even forgotten that the citizen exists as such. There is the unwholesome, and to some extent, degrading habit of thinking always in terms of communities and never in terms of citizens'[4]... These positions logically led to a conception of a secular state as one that stays away from religion per se. It distances itself from all religions and in this manner encourages their limitation to a private sphere; it presses for the narrowing of religion to the activity of religious worship and it assiduously replaces respect for religion with building nationalist citizens. India was engaged in creating a modern nation state and in this enterprise, religion, an obscurantist and divisive force, had no place...

The second position on secularism, exactly opposite to the first, was that no links between the state and religion should be permitted, not because this would weaken the state, but because it would demean religion. Religion, a system of absolute truth, could not be made subject to the whims of changing majorities by allowing the democratic state to have a say in religious affairs. Like the first, the third position—

---

[3]Rao, B. Shiva. *The Framing of India's Constitution: Select Documents—Vol. II*, Government of India Press, Nasik, 1968, p. 16.
[4]Ibid pp. 62–63.

which we call the equal-respect theory of secularism—also began with the principle of religious liberty, but held that in a society like India where religion was such an important part of most people's lives, this principle entailed not that the state stay away from all religions equally, but that it respect all religions alike.

In this view, instead of distancing itself from all religions or tolerating them equivalently as sets of superstitions which could be indulged in as long as they remained a private affair, a secular state based its dealings with religion on an equal respect to all religions. Since religion was, for most Indians, a way of life and, therefore, essential to their identity, how could a people's state be founded on a kind of secularism contemptuous of religion. One's identity was not something which was easily changeable, and for these members to forcibly replace religion as the basis of one's identity with the state was an attack on the autonomy of individuals. In addition, most important religions contained principles of toleration within themselves since by definition, religious belief had to be voluntary. If the state allowed a public sphere to religion this would not automatically lead to inter-sectarian strife, as all great religions of the world preached forbearance of other faiths. J.B. Kripalani defined toleration as the acceptance, to some extent, of someone's beliefs as good for him, and argued that it was because the no-concern theory was based on a doctrine of intolerance that it confined religion to the private realm. On the other hand a state which respected all religions was educating its citizens in principles of toleration: 'We have to respect each other's faith. We have to respect it as having an element of truth'.[5] Jaya Prakash Narayan added that it was only when religion was used to serve socio-economic and political interests, that there was communal violence. What needed to be done in the interests of secularism was to incorporate an article in the Constitution prohibiting the use of religious institutions for political purposes or the setting up of political organisations on a religious basis.[6] It was not religion per se but its politicisation which engendered violence in the modern state. The no-concern and equal-respect positions on secularism clashed constantly during the debates in the Constituent Assembly as the question of secularism cropped up in discussions around innumerable articles...

Linguistic or Religious Minorities

The differences over secularism were also clearly apparent in the controversy over whether a secular state permits the recognition of religious minorities along with linguistic minorities. On the one hand, Jaya Prakash Narayan held that the 'secularisation of general education...necessary for the growth of a national outlook and unity'[7] required

---

[5] *Constituent Assembly Debates—Vol. X*, Lok Sabha Secretariat, 2014, p. 435.
[6] Rao, B. Shiva. *The Framing of India's Constitution: A Study*, Government of India Press, Nasik, 1968, p. 266.
[7] Ibid p. 276.

that the cultural and educational rights guaranteed in the Constitution should be confined only to linguistic minorities... Rajkumari Amrit Kaur had similarly proposed that religious minorities not be allowed to set up separate educational institutions, nor state aid be provided to these institutions...

Uniform Civil Code

The first article that we take up with reference to citizenship in a secular state is that on the uniform civil code. Both K.M. Munshi's and B.R. Ambedkar's draft articles of March 1947 on justiciable rights contained clauses referring indirectly to a uniform civil code, Munshi's proposal stated that: 'No civil or criminal court shall, in adjudicating any matter or executing any order recognise any custom or usage imposing any civil disability on any person on the ground of his caste, status, religion, race or language'.[8] Ambedkar wrote that the subjects of the Indian state shall have the right 'to claim full and equal benefit of all laws and proceedings for the security of persons and property as is enjoyed by other subjects regardless of any usage or custom based on religion and be subject to like punishment, pains and penalties and to none other'.[9] By March 30, however, the

---

[8]Rao, B. Shiva. *The Framing of India's Constitution: Select Documents Documents—Vol. II*, Government of India Press, Nasik, 1968, p. 79.
[9]Ibid p. 89.

Fundamental Rights Sub-Committee had decided to make the uniform civil code a directive principle of state policy. In her letter of March 31, Rajkumari Amrit Kaur emphasised the importance of the uniform civil code and called it 'very vital to social progress'.[10] In a much more strongly worded note of April 14, Amrit Kaur, along with Hansa Mehta and M.R. Masani, wrote that '(o)ne of the factors that has kept India back from advancing to nationhood has been the existence of personal laws based on religion which keep the nation divided into watertight compartments in many aspects of life'[11], and demanded that the provision regarding the uniform civil code be transferred from the chapter on directive principles to that on fundamental rights. This position was opposed by other members of the Constituent Assembly, such as Mohamed Ismail Saheb, supported by B. Pocker Sahib, who wanted to include a right to one's personal law in the fundamental right to religion. law'. ...This must be done if the right to religious practice was to have any reality because the 'right to follow personal law is part of the way of life of those people who are following such laws; it is part of their religion and part of their culture'.[12] Mahboob Ali Baig Bahadur said, 'People seem to think that under a secular state, there must be a common law observed by its citizens in all matters including matters of their daily

---

[10] Ibid p. 147.
[11] Ibid p. 162.
[12] *Constituent Assembly Debates—Vol. VII*, Lok Sabha Secretariat, 2014, p. 540.

life, their language, their culture, their personal laws. This is not the correct way to look at the secular state. In a secular state, citizens belonging to different communities must have the freedom to practise their own religion, observe their own life and their personal laws should be applied to them'.[13](41) These members were opposed to the setting up of a uniform civil code. An intermediate position was that the establishment of the uniform civil code must be done slowly, with the consent of all communities. Similar to this position was that of K.M. Munshi's—who now, surprisingly, wanted to narrow the definition of religious practice. He pointed out that the personal law of Hindus was discriminatory against women and contravened an Indian citizen's right to equality. Therefore, 'religion must be restricted to spheres which legitimately appertain to religion, and the rest of life must be regulated, unified and modified in such a manner that we may evolve, as early as possible, a strong and consolidated nation.'[14] Ambedkar can also be put in this group since he supported the inclusion of the uniform civil code in the directive principles but said that the code would only apply to those who wanted it to apply to them.

---

[13]Ibid p. 544.
[14]Ibid p. 548.

Political Safeguards for Minorities

Simultaneously with discussing the kind of religious rights permitted by secularism, the Constituent Assembly's members also debated the political rights of minorities in a secular state. The Minorities Sub-Committee based itself on its members' responses to a short questionnaire on safeguards for minorities prepared by K.M. Munshi, and on Ambedkar's suggested safeguards for the scheduled castes. Munshi's questionnaire consisted of six queries on the nature and scope of political, economic, religious, educational and cultural safeguards for a minority at the centre and the provinces in the new constitution, on the machinery to ensure these safeguards, and on whether these safeguards would be temporary or permanent. Ambedkar's draft contained a section on 'provisions for the protection of minorities' demanding that the representatives of the different minorities in the cabinet be elected by members of each minority community in the legislature, as well as the establishment of a superintendent of minority affairs. Although only the scheduled castes were specifically named as a minority by Ambedkar, he did assume the inclusion of other minorities when he wrote that the share of the scheduled castes in the reserved seats in the legislatures or the services would not be at the cost of the share of the other minorities.

Religious Instruction in Educational Institutions

When this clause was discussed in the Constituent Assembly on August 30, 1947, it was sought to be amended by Renuka Ray to read as follows: 'No denominational religious instruction shall be provided in schools maintained by the state'.[15] Radhakrishnan explained the reasoning behind such an amendment: 'We are a multi-religious state and therefore we have to be impartial and give uniform treatment to the different religions; but if institutions maintained by the state, that is, administered, controlled and financed by the state are permitted to impart religious instruction of a denominational kind, we are violating the first principle of our Constitution.'[16] Here we see at its clearest, one understanding of secularism: impartiality to all religions means that the state must stay away from all religions... Diametrically opposite was the argument of Mohamed Ismail who believed that 'the stability of society as well as of the state could be secured through a moral background which religion alone could provide, and it was in the interest of the state itself to give children a grounding in religion.'[17] Thus there ought to be no bar on religious instruction in educational institutions, not even in those run exclusively by the state, as long as no one was compelled to accept

---

[15]Rao, B. Shiva. *The Framing of India's Constitution: A Study*, Government of India Press, Nasik, 1968, p. 263.
[16]Ibid.
[17]Ibid p. 269.

such instruction. If religious instruction was imparted in this manner by the state, it would in no way contravene the neutrality or the secular nature of the state... If on the one hand, the Constitution stated that minorities were entitled to state aid and recognition to their freely run educational institutions, then how could it also ban religious instruction in state aided institutions. The only solution was to say that no pupil could be forced to attend religious instruction in state aided schools.

Conclusion

Ever since the Romantics, we have learnt that contradictions are not a problem; they capture better the complexity of anything. But surely a Constitution—a legal document—has to obey canons of consistency? Both the no-concern and equal-respect positions on secularism, when constructed strictly logically by Rajkumari Amrit Kaur and B. Pocker Sahib, had few takers in the Constituent Assembly. Most members felt that neither a position demanding a right only to religious worship, the recognition by the state of no minority, whether religious, linguistic or sexual, the establishment of a uniform civil code, no political safeguards for any minority and no religious instruction in any state schools, nor its mirror opposite—claiming a right to the practice of religion, state recognition for religious as well as linguistic minorities, personal laws to be included in fundamental rights, political safeguards for all religious minorities, and religious instruction in state schools—captured the requirements of secularism in 'the context of India's social diversity. The first position suffered from a 'statist' conception of nationalism, 'giving an inescapably 'statist' orientation to the very conception of any political unity across religious communities and other social divisions'.[18] It wished to establish a direct link between the citizens and the state, by weakening all other loyalties and commitments of individuals. Apart from neglecting the importance of cultural and religious considerations to one's identity, this conception of secularism reflected a naive belief in the benign nature of the modern democratic state. The second position was weakened by its failure to provide any avenues for dissent within different religious communities. Much more important were two intermediate positions in the Constituent Assembly, one of which sought, for instance, to combine the right to religious worship and to a uniform civil code with political reservation for minorities. This position lost, and the one which is reflected in the actual articles of the Constitution, defined the right to religion broadly as the right to religious practice, but refused to grant political safeguards to religious minorities. Today, we are inclined to favour a conception of a secular state as an equal respecter of all religions. Can the Constituent Assembly debates throw

---

[18]Sen, Amartya. 'Secularism and Its Discontents', K. Basu and S. Subramahmyam, *Unravelling the Nation: Sectarian Conflict and India's Secular Identity*, Penguin Books, New Delhi, 1996, p. 26.

any light on whether this conception requires not only that religion be defined broadly by the state, but also that minorities must be granted political safeguards. Is this the only way that the state can prevent itself from becoming a Hindu state or will this added provision worsen the situation for Indian democracy?

Excerpts reproduced from the article published in *Economic and Political Weekly* (27 July–2 August 2002) with the permission of the author, who is a professor at the Centre for Political Studies, School of Social Sciences in JNU, Delhi.

Index

42nd Amendment, 34, 47
2002 Gujarat riots, 5, 145

Aam Aadmi Party (AAP), 53
Adityanath, Yogi, 81
Advani, L.K., 144
Aligarh Muslim University (AMU), 32, 58, 70, 80, 116, 119, 129
All India Congress Committee, 75
All India Majlis-e-Ittehadul Muslimeen (AIMIM), 10, 80, 104, 105, 120
All-India Muslim League (Muslim League), x, xiii, 45, 83, 92, 93, 94, 95, 96, 99, 105
All India Muslim Personal Law Board (AIMPLB), 39

Ambedkar, B.R., 46, 102, 112, 123, 140, 181
ANHAD (Act Now for Harmony and Democracy), 68
Apoorvanand, 68
Atatürk, Kemal, 29

Babri Masjid, 12, 16, 32, 38, 39, 40, 49, 78, 80, 115, 128, 144, 149, 156
Bahadur, Mahboob Ali Baig, 182
Bhagwat, Mohan, 27
Bhargava, Rajeev, 7, 154, 157
Bhartiya Janata Party (BJP), x, 3, 4, 10, 12, 13, 20, 29, 35, 37, 45, 54, 62, 63, 64, 66, 67, 71, 77, 81, 88, 89, 90, 93, 106,

115, 116, 120, 130, 137, 145, 146, 147

Centre for the Study of Developing Societies (CSDS), 7
Chandhoke, Neera, 5, 50, 154
Church of England, 24, 155, 171
Citizenship (Amendment) Act (CAA), 2019, xiv, 34, 52, 53, 55, 57, 58, 59, 60, 61, 62, 64, 66, 67, 68, 69, 74, 75, 77, 79, 81, 84, 85, 88, 89, 90, 91, 107, 116, 130, 137, 138
Congress party, x, xi, xiii, 3, 9, 35, 36, 37, 38, 39, 40, 49, 56, 92, 94, 95, 96, 97, 98, 99, 100, 110, 115, 127, 149
COVID-19, 71, 72, 73, 74
cultural pluralism, 117, 123

Deshpande, Pushparaj, 75, 78

Emergency, 34, 35, 36, 37
Erdoğan, Recep Tayyip, 29

Gandhi, Indira, 34, 36, 37
Gandhi, Rahul, 14, 66, 89
Ganga–Jamuni tehzeeb, 4, 131, 132, 133
Garg, Nand Kishore, 71
Godhra, 145

Golwalkar, M.S., 84, 85, 87, 88, 103
Good Friday Agreement, 43

Hameed, Syeda, 68
Hasan, Faizul, 80
Hashmi, Shabnam, 68
Hashmi, Sohail, 56, 139, 141
Hegde, Sanjay, 71
Hidayatullah, Ghulam Hussain, 93
Hinduization, 15, 23
Hindu nationalist, x, 2, 9, 12, 66, 91, 112, 120, 137, 144, 153
Hindu Rashtra, 9, 11, 12, 17, 18, 19, 22, 23, 27, 51, 84, 86, 87, 95, 106, 136, 154, 170, 171, 173
Hindu Right, 3, 5, 13, 40, 65, 96, 100, 118, 119, 144
Hindutva, 12, 27, 80, 83, 86, 91, 96, 115, 124, 125, 130, 133, 136
Housing Discrimination Project, 33
Huq, A.K. Fazlul, 93, 94
hyper-nationalism, 82

Imam, Sharjeel, 58, 66
Indian Union Muslim League (IUML), 105
intra-religious domination, 159,

162, 163, 165
Islamization, 29

Jaffrelot, Christophe, 5
Jamia Millia Islamia (JMI) University, 58, 59, 63, 67, 116, 130
Jawaharlal Nehru University (JNU), 58, 76, 126, 188
Jazbi, Moin Ahsan, 143
Jinnah, Mohammed Ali, x, 21, 43, 44, 45, 46, 64, 66, 83, 85, 96, 97, 98, 99, 100, 103, 105, 124, 136, 137
Jolly, Vijay, 63
Jung, Najeeb, 56
Justice and Development Party (AKP), 29, 30

Karavan-e-Mohabbat, 68
Kaur, Amrit, 181, 182, 186
Kejriwal, Arvind, 53, 54, 66, 89
Khan, Aamir, 116
Khan, Agha, 99
Kripalani, J.B., 179

Lahore Resolution, 94
love jihad, 116, 137

majoritarianism, xi, 15, 27, 34, 61, 76, 106, 108, 112, 115, 133, 136, 137, 144, 152, 168

Malviya, Amit, 62, 64
Mander, Harsh, 57, 68
Mein Kampf, 84
minorityism, 36, 40, 166
Modi, Narendra, 7, 13, 60, 62, 89, 106, 145, 147
Mohani, Maulana Hasrat, 140
Munshi, K.M., 181, 183, 184
Muslim question, 5, 152
Mustafa, Faizan, 17, 154, 170

Narayan, Jaya Prakash, 180
National Population Register (NPR), 57, 59, 69
National Register of Citizens (NRC), 59, 61, 66, 107
Nehru–Gandhi family, 14
Nehru, Jawaharlal, 2, 58, 110, 119
North-West Frontier Province (NWFP), 93, 94
Nussbaum, Martha, 5

Owaisi, Akbaruddin, 80
Owaisi, Asaduddin, 10, 105

Pant, G.B., 178
Patel, Sardar Vallabhbhai, 92, 102
Political Secularism, 160
Prasad, Rajendra, 46, 120
Preamble, 47, 56, 110, 114, 140, 175

pseudo-secularism, x, 3, 128, 144, 148

Quit India Movement, 94, 95, 96

Rahman, Ziaur, 28, 173
Ram Janambhoomi, 39
Ram Mandir, 12, 38, 49, 115, 144
Ram rajya, 131
Rao, P.V. Narasimha, 35, 38
Rashtriya Janata Dal (RJD), 37
religious apartheid, 155
Religious Nationalism, 82
Rushdie, Salman, 1, 16

Sabarmati Express, 145
Sadavarte, Zen Gunratan, 65
Sahib, B. Pocker, 182, 186
Sahmat, 68
Sahni, Amit, 71
Samajwadi Party (SP), 37
Samruddha Bharat Foundation, 75
Sangh Parivar, 12, 78, 80, 144, 150

Savarkar, V.D., 83, 136
Shah, Amit, 66, 67, 89
Shah, K.T., 46
Siddiqui, Shahid, 147
Singh, Bhagat, 140
Singh, Jaswant, 45
Singh, Manmohan, 35, 41
Sultanpuri, Majrooh, 117

Tablighi Jamaat, 116
Tharoor, Shashi, 56, 133
theocracy, xii, 3, 11, 19, 23, 24, 26, 44
The Satanic Verses, 16, 49
triple talaq, 56, 156
Turkman Gate, 36

UK Equality Act, 24
United Nations Educational, Scientific and Cultural Organization (UNESCO), 29

Vajpayee, Atal Behari, 145
Vishwa Hindu Parishad (VHP), 39

www.ingramcontent.com/pod-product-compliance
Lightning Source LLC
Chambersburg PA
CBHW020232170426
43201CB00007B/397